History & Guide

Truro

Christine Parnell

History & Guide

Truro

Christine Parnell

TEMPUS

Truro Cathedral from the south, taken during the week that it was announced that the plans originally drawn up by J.L. Pearson for a cloister and the connection of thecathedral to the old cathedral school building were to be revived.

First published 2002

Tempus Publishing Ltd
The Mill, Brimscombe Port
Stroud, Gloucestershire GL5 2QG

British Library Cataloguing in Publication Data.
A catalogue record for this book is available from the British Library.

ISBN 0 7524 2640 0

Typesetting and origination by Tempus Publishing.
Printed in Great Britain by Midway Colour Print, Wiltshire

Contents

Preface & Acknowledgements

I have been interested in the history of Truro for a long time. In fact, soon after starting at the Truro County Grammar School for Girls and being given a test on the history of Cornwall, followed a short time later by another test about Truro, both subjects became hobbies of mine. It is impossible to remember where I learned the things that I discuss in this book but certainly the fact that Mr H.L. Douch – curator of the museum at that time – took several of us on a walk round the town, pointing out things of interest and giving us the historical facts, gave me a good start. To refresh my memory I dipped in and out of all the books listed in the bibliography.

The walk is one which Arthur J. Lyne introduced me to. During his forty years as secretary of the Truro Old Cornwall Society he used to take interested groups of people round the town, and now that I have been the secretary for several years the task has fallen to me.

I must thank all those who willingly gave up their time to help in searching out photographs and telling me various anecdotes that they thought might be of interest I would like to mention Pamela Glasson, Arnold and Violet Hodge, David and Denise Parnell and Simon Vage. David Thomas helped photograph some of the city's treasures with the kind permission of Russell Holden, the Town Clerk. As usual I must thank my husband Peter who has taken photographs, drawn pictures and trailed round the town with me checking that the details for the walk were accurate and that I would not be leading anyone astray. I hope I have not forgotten anyone but if I have please accept my apologies.

Christine Parnell
September 2002

CHAPTER 1

Truro's First Charter

It is surprising that a small town deep in the south-west of the country has so much history but Truro, nestling in a valley beside three rivers which together form the Truro River and become the Fal, has had an interesting past.

Who knows how a town really comes into being? Much can be gleaned from old records but much must be guessed, based on logic and knowledge of history. Wayside crosses are scattered throughout Cornwall, marking the tracks used by pilgrims, traders and wayfarers. Truro's own cross is found in the area outside the west door of the cathedral, known as High Cross. What is known is that 700 years ago the burgage plots turned sharply at this point, most probably to accommodate the cross which already stood there and it is here that Truro is believed to have its origins.

The view down river from Kenwyn.

An aerial view of the city in 1986.

The town grew up on the trade route crossing the county from the River Gannel at Newquay to the Fal. The quickest route went straight to Malpas (pronounced Mopus) possibly the Mal Pas of Tristan and Iseult. Those who came further down into the valley to break their journey found themselves in a settlement between two rivers and marked by the wayside cross. The fertile valley had a high ridge behind it and faced the river leading to Falmouth and the sea, an ideal place to settle although some areas were damp and marshy and fog and mist tended to collect in the dip.

No one really knows the meaning of the word 'Truro'. For many years the origin was thought to be 'three roads'. Charles Henderson believed that Pydar Street was older than the town itself, and this road, once called Strete Pydar, came down to the cross from the old administrative area of the hundred of Pydar and the direction of the Gannel. The other two roads would have been Kenwyn Street – a name applied to various streets at different times – leading to the Falmouth and Helston area or to Penzance and finally St Clement Street for roads to St Austell.

These days, however, it is believed more likely that Truro is derived from 'Tri-veru' or 'Try-weru' which appeared in documents of the thirteenth century and conveys the meaning three rivers, as suggested by H.L. Douch. Two of those rivers are well known to all: the Kenwyn, whose old name was Dowr Ithy, which flows through the leats, under River Street and once under the West Bridge and the River Allen which runs through the town under the old East Bridge, now Old Bridge. The third river is not so well known although the Truro Glass Company have called their headquarters Glasteinan House in its honour, suggesting that their glass is as clear and sparkling as the little river. It is little more than a trickle these days which wanders under Tregolls Road and the Trafalgar area to drain out into the river near Boscawen Bridge.

No one is sure of the origins of the castle at Truro but it was definitely in place during King Stephen's tempestuous reign. During the civil war with his cousin Matilda many castles sprang up round the country, known as adulterine castles and this was perhaps one of them. Possibly an old Celtic style of fortification once stood on the site, an earthwork with ramparts and ditches which could later have been adapted and built up with stone. To understand how the castle and its occupants affected the rise of Truro it is necessary to know a little of the background history.

King Stephen had made William Fitz Richard, the lord of Cardinham, his lieutenant in Cornwall but when Fitz Richard's daughter married Matilda's half brother, Reginald, he decided to switch allegiance and fight for Matilda. In 1140 Reginald declared himself Earl of Cornwall and the lands which they already held as well as any taken subsequently were all held in Matilda's name. Stephen, incensed, rode into the county with his army, seized the castles that Reginald and William held and made one of his own men, Alan of Brittany, the Earl of Cornwall.

One of the men in Alan's service was Richard de Lucy, the man credited with granting Truro its first charter and bringing the town into being. As a reward for his services he was granted some of the land confiscated from Reginald and the lord of Cardinham which included Truro and the castle, at this time just a circular building on a mound, not a large or grand building but perhaps something along the lines of the one which still exists in Launceston. In 1840, 700 years later, the ground was being cleared for a new cattle market and the remains of thick stone walls were uncovered, though much of the stone had disappeared years before to be used elsewhere.

For Richard de Lucy to prosper, it was necessary for the townsfolk to prosper and they came to the town to carry on their trade. Richard encouraged them by allowing those who settled in the free burgage plots

The top of the original wheel-headed cross, which has been placed on a new shaft in High Cross.

to become free men. No written record of his charter exists today but it is believed to have been granted in 1153. Richard was appointed Chief Justicier to Stephen shortly before the king's death in 1154 and when Matilda's son Henry II came to the throne, he confirmed Richard de Lucy in his appointment. So trustworthy was he that Henry called him 'Richard the Loyal'. Henry also granted a favour to his mother's half brother Reginald and once more Reginald became Earl of Cornwall.

It was around 1173 that Reginald confirmed de Lucy's earlier charter which had given the town the right to manage its own affairs and hold a court. It also had the right of 'Infangenethef' an old word which gave the townspeople the right to hang their own thieves. The confirmation added three further rights. Freedom from fair and market tolls in other towns in the county, freedom from the jurisdiction of the hundred and county courts and the right to seize the property of their fellow burgesses for debt.

Strangely it has never been proved whether Richard de Lucy ever lived in his castle in Truro. He may never even have visited it. It would be nice though to imagine him living here among the people who made the rise of the borough possible by their hard work and endeavours and glancing out of his castle on the hill from time to time, feeling proud of his achievement.

Much later the burgesses reinforced their charter yet again by buying confirmation of it from Edward I but it was in 1153 when Richard de Lucy first granted a charter to the infant town which was springing up outside his castle walls that Truro really came into being.

Glasteinan House, named after Truro's third river.

CHAPTER 2

From the coming of the Friars to the Black Death

By the middle of the thirteenth century, Truro, along with many other towns, had an order of monks arrive to settle in one of the poorer areas. Truro welcomed the black friars or Dominican monks, an order whose influence lives on in the name of St Dominic Street. The Dominicans had only reached England in 1221 and for them to have arrived and settled in the town so soon underlines Truro's importance. They lived in the triangle of land between the river and Kenwyn Street. St Dominic Street might have been the boundary of their land but the old Lake's Pottery, now gone, was further up Chapel Hill and was thought by Mr and Mrs Lake to have been a pottery even in the time of the monks.

Although no one is certain exactly where their monastic buildings were, the cobbles in what used to be the blacksmith's shop at 108 Kenwyn Street were laid down by the friars. The cobbles are still there, although sadly now covered over, and it is thought that their chapel stood at the back of 107 Kenwyn Street, for many years the site of the Western Inn. The land which stretched down to the river behind Kenwyn Street was a fertile area known as the Friary Meadow, so one can be fairly certain that that land at least was used by the friars.

Behind 10 Kenwyn Street of today (there has been a re-numbering in recent years which has only slightly altered the positions of the numbers), on a wall behind British Telecom is a stone face reputed to be a carving of a monk, possibly the abbot who was buried on the site. Legend says that a hawthorne tree grew on his grave and, as it was cut down in 1985 by British Telecom, the staff have supposedly lived in fear of the death foretold by an ancient curse. The tree still survives though; an offshoot of the tree is still growing at the rear of No. 10 (a restaurant) and as no untoward deaths have occurred, perhaps all is still well. However some members of staff who have worked on the site over the years have been uneasy working there, sometimes feeling a presence and at least one lady has recently said that she believes she has seen 'something'.

Further up the road in the direction of St Dominic Street was a holy well reputed to have effected marvellous cures from its stream of pure water and to be particularly effective for sore eyes. The friars were also an order of missionaries, so as well as tending to the medical needs of the people, they were also preaching to them. It is possible they were the ones who set up the wayside cross as a focus for their religion and a place from which to preach.

Ralph Reskymer from St Mawgan in Meneage gave land to the friary in 1462 and let it be known that his ancestors had founded the establishment. Whether that was so or whether it had been founded by royalty, as Richard II stated, is unclear but the order remained in Truro and flourished until the Dissolution of the Monasteries in the late 1530s.

Not long after the Dominicans arrival in Truro, an important person paid them a visit. In September 1259, Bishop Bronescombe came down from Exeter to consecrate their chapel, located, as we know, somewhere in today's Kenwyn Street. As it was such a long and arduous journey from Exeter, it was just as well to make good use of the bishop while he was in town. He also re-dedicated the church at Kenwyn and dedicated the chapel of St Mary in the town.

Kenwyn church, named after a female saint, St Keyne, was the parish church and already old by the time of the bishop's visit. St Keyne and her women had settled by the ancient well and founded the church about 100 years before St Augustine brought Christianity to the country. It was obviously either rebuilt or largely repaired by 1259, hence the re-dedication by the bishop. The problem with Kenwyn church was that it was uphill out of the newly grown town and hard work for the young and old to reach it. The newly dedicated chapel of Our Lady (St Mary's) in the centre by the old cross was much easier to get to and in time would take over as the parish church and become independent of its older

Opposite: Kenwyn Street looking down towards the site of the old friary.

Kenwyn church.

St Keyne's Well at Kenwyn church.

neighbour on the hill. The other church in the vicinity was down by the waterside at St Clement. It was probably built around 1249 on the site of an older chapel and served the manor of Moresk as a parish church. The manor was one of the biggest in Cornwall and took in the area up as far as St Erme, with the River Allen as its boundary on the west and the Tresillian River on the east. Part of Truro was included in the parish until the beginning of the nineteenth century, roughly the Mitchell Hill area of today, with St Austell Street and St Clement Street as well. Although the present church is believed to have been dedicated in 1249, ten years before Bishop Bronescombe came to Truro, the parish booklet tells us that the Earls of Cornwall lived at Condurro before the Norman Conquest and it was probably one of them who founded and endowed the church.

So now the borough had its own church, possibly it had been in existence for some time and served by priests from Kenwyn before being

Opposite: The face of a monk at the site where it is believed the friars had their cemetery.

15

St Clement's church.

recognised officially, and there may also have been another chapel in the town. A group of traders had formed themselves into a guild known as the Fraternity of St Nicholas, after whom St Nicholas Street is named. Charles Henderson quotes a deed of 1278 which refers to the guild as being the 'overlord' of some of the houses in that street. It would have been usual for such a guild to possess a chapel and it is possible that they did in fact have one near the West Bridge.

Another chapel which crops up during the medieval era is one which had an unusual dedication to the 'blessed Mary of Portell'. This was a very uncommon dedication and Truro was the only place in the country where the sect had a chapel. Originally venerated in Rome in the sixth century it is possible that the dedication was brought back to Truro by an adventurous merchant. The chapel was most probably situated by the Old Bridge of today, the East Bridge then, which if it had already been built would have been a very new structure. Even today the name still exists, as the Roman Catholic church in Truro is 'Our Lady of the Portal and St Piran'.

With the settlement of the friars, the rise of the merchant guild and the borough finally having its own church (100 years after the foundation of the borough) Truro was a thriving community. Having a chapel near the East Bridge and possibly another by the West Bridge was a sure way to keep the bridges in good repair with money from indulgences sold at the chapel helping towards their upkeep.

Opposite: Medieval East Bridge, now Old Bridge over the River Allen.

Millstone in the ground at Bice's Court, off Kenwyn Street.

The rivers in Truro meant that there was plenty of water to power the mills and keep the wheels turning. The town mill was where River Street and St Nicholas Street meet, facing towards Victoria Square. This was a very old mill necessary to the castle and powered by a leat – later called Tregeare Water. In Truro the pathway to Victoria Gardens is known as The Leats, as it runs alongside the water channel. The granite gutters in Boscawen Street also carry water from the rivers , and they too are known as the leats. At Carvedras another mill pounded away for the friars although, as there is a millstone set into the floor at Bices Court (off Kenwyn Street) they probably had another mill lower down the river. The Duchy Mill worked for the manor of Moresk and another mill on the River Allen was the manorial mill and remnants of its old mill pool can be found behind the cathedral. Other mills at intervals along the two rivers provided power and helped the economy of the young town.

So at this time, the early part of the fourteenth century, the West Bridge would have been a fairly new structure, narrow and with stepping stones beside it. The East Bridge would also have been fairly new with fording places where it was easy to cross, one of which is now the site of the New Bridge. Much of the land between the rivers was divided into stitches, narrow strips of land running down to one or other river with the ruined castle on the hill and the mother church of Kenwyn further up still. Down in the valley was the new church of St Mary's, beside the manorial mill. The monastic buildings were away over on the other side of the West Bridge with possibly a guild chapel in St Nicholas Street. Beyond the buildings of the friars, where Kenwyn Street ascends out of the valley and where Chapel Hill now is, was a leper colony. The disease was rife and there was no cure for the unfortunates who contracted it. Fingers or toes could rot and drop off as could the nose or other facial features. Not only would the affected person look horrific but if the damage turned gangrenous they would have a dreadful stench. It was customary to have leper houses near roads so that travellers could be asked for alms and many people left legacies to the leper colonies for the relief of sufferers.

Truro was a thriving town, not large but confined to the valley beneath the old castle with access to the sea from its several quays. The only threat appeared to be from Newham where members of the de Pridyas family had ambitions to raise their manor to borough status. However, by 1300 Thomas de Pridyas had bought the half of the manor and borough which had come to John de Ripariis, husband of one of Richard de Lucy's two granddaughters and so had no need to promote Newham to the detriment of Truro.

Thus Truro thrived until a new and much more sinister threat to its being arose. Throughout Europe people were dying in their tens of thousands, there was no cure and no escape. The Black Death had arrived.

CHAPTER 3
From the Black Death to the Dissolution of the Monasteries

By 1348 the Black Death had reached Normandy. Soon it had crossed the channel and Dorset had an outbreak of the dreaded disease. It did not take long for it to reach Devon and soon after Cornwall became infected. Death followed within a few hours of black pustules appearing and the unfortunate victim starting to spit blood. The towns were hit worst as people lived clustered together in unsanitary conditions, often with open drains running through the streets, helping the plague spread like wildfire. It is possible that Cornwall was actually less severely affected than many areas, as many of the people lived in scattered hamlets but nevertheless it is estimated that one third of the population died.

It was particularly noticeable that many of the churches lost their priests, dedicated men who went out among their parishoners and tended the sick. The young and the old stood very little chance of survival. Such was the devastation that the old order of things was gone forever.

Many land holdings became vacant. Rotting carcasses of animals lay unburied in the fields, people had either died or fled from the pestilence and left animals untended. It soon became obvious that the old medieval system had broken down. Lords of the manor found themselves short of labour and the labourers discovered that they could ask for their freedom and if they did not get it they could simply move away to another manor where their labour would be welcomed and more money paid to keep them happy. The little rhyme, 'When Adam delved and Eve span, Who was then a gentleman?' was heard throughout the land as the common people realised their worth.

The plague had also had a devastating effect on the tin industry. There was a lack of manpower, consequently a slump in the amount of tin produced. Gone were the record coinages of 1337 (over 700 tons) and it was the end of the century before such amounts were seen again, nevertheless the Black Prince, the first Duke of Cornwall, still demanded as much labour expended and money brought in as before.

Truro was in a bad way and she was not alone, as all the other towns in Cornwall were suffering as well. Although the war with the French being waged by Edward III had briefly been interrupted by the Black Death it continued as before once the worst of the plague was over. His loyal subjects were still expected to ferry supplies to the coast where the army was defending the country. In 1376 the Black Prince died followed by his father, Edward III, a year later and the war with France abated, easing things for the people.

Although the burden had lessened, Truro was in poor financial shape. In 1378 the burgesses petitioned Richard II to reduce their taxes. He caused his sheriff to make enquiries and was told that the town was indeed impoverished and the taxes were reduced which eased the plight of the people.

One way of raising money in medieval times was the granting of indulgences. These were granted by a bishop, or indeed the pope himself, to reduce the amount of time one had to spend in purgatory after death. A repentant sinner could give alms at a shrine that had been granted the power to sell indulgences and the sinner, usually on a pilgrimage as a way of expiating his sin, could benefit by having some of his punishment in purgatory reduced. The money raised by the sale of indulgences helped to pay for the upkeep of the shrine and perhaps some of the surrounding area such as a road or bridge.

By 1420 a chapel to St George had been built at the top of Chapel Hill and in 1427 the pope granted an indulgence of 100 days to pilgrims visiting it on certain feast days. To spend that much less time in purgatory was quite an attraction and people would have parted with their hard-earned money gladly. Down in the town, the chapel of St Mary was by this time 150 years old and in 1400 was able to sell indulgences, probably to help keep it in a state of good repair. It was a good way of having money available to maintain buildings and was one of the ways in which the East and West Bridges were kept in good condition.

Despite the lack of manpower and the poor financial state of the borough, life carried on after the plague and it was around 1350 that a new row of properties was built in the town. Middle Row, as it was called, ran through the middle of what is Boscawen Street today. It consisted of a row of houses and shops but included a market house at the western end of the row, near the site of Littlewoods today. This building had pillars supporting an upper floor where the burgesses met and all council business was conducted. The room underneath was used as a shop and the building survived for a good twenty years after the rest of the row was demolished in the nineteenth century. Near the other end of the row was the prison close to the coinage hall.

It was in 1327 that Truro was granted the status of stannary town. It had been proclaimed by the Lord Mayor of London on the order of the king much to the dismay of Lostwithiel where the townsfolk jealously guarded their right to be the only coinage town in Cornwall. They now had to share that privilege with Truro and in later years both of them fought unsuccessfully to stop the right being extended to Helston and Bodmin. In 1351 the Duke of Cornwall's steward was instructed to build or buy a house for the coinage and the coinage hall was built, but not joined to, the far end of Middle Row. It remained there until demolition in 1848.

The coinage was traditionally held twice a year at midsummer and Michaelmas and would have been quite an occasion. All sorts of people would have come to witness the events starting with the blocks of tin being brought to the coinagehall and piled up ready for assaying. They would already have had the mark of the smelter on them and, if they passed the test of purity, the mark of the duchy would be added to show that the quality was assured and the tax paid. At noon, the steward, the controller and the receiver took their seats facing the King's beam, the hammer with which to stamp the arms of the duchy and the weights were unpacked from their sealed bags and the blocks of tin were weighed in turn. The peizer (the weigher) shouted out the weight which the three men noted. The assay master chiselled a small piece of tin from the corner (coin) of the block and did a quality test on it and, if satisfied, the controller would stamp the hammer with the arms of the duchy on to the block. The town would have been bustling with porters who heaved the blocks of tin around, the tinners themselves and the people who intended to purchase the tin. No doubt a certain amount of smuggling went on, small amounts of tin could be carried in a pocket and sold to any willing pewterer but on the whole the crowds coming to the town, all needing food, drink and lodging was good for the economy of the town. Much later, in the eighteenth century, reference is made to celebrating during the coinage and standing treat at 'ye Ship', 'Kings Head', 'Red Lyon and ye Coffee House at Truro'.

The pillars which used to support the upper storey of the old Market House in Middle Row, now incorporated into the City Inn, Pydar Street.

Members of Truro Old Cornwall Society celebrating the eightieth anniversary of their founding on 15 June 2002. From left to right: David May, Betty May, Joan Alwyn, Lorna Cave, Eleanor Knee, Kate Dickinson, John Bowden. Front right: Mervyn Steeds, Joan Steeds, Violet Hodge, Arnold Hodge.

The friars still played an important part in the life of the people. In 1354 when the Black Prince paid his first visit to Cornwall some of the friars headed to Restormel Castle to see him. Many people went to catch a glimpse of him during his two-week stay but the friars were some of the lucky ones who came away with a gift. They had permission to take ten oak trees from his park to use as beams in the building of their new house. They also received many bequests over the years. One was from John Meger, or Magor, a pewterer who left money for them to say masses for his soul. As far as is known, he had been born in Truro, if not Truro certainly Cornwall, but had gone to London and done well, becoming a member of parliament and a freeman of London. He made his money by selling Cornish commodities but what those commodities were is uncertain. However he had not forgotten his Cornish roots and remembered family and friends in his will and made many local bequests.

Despite a raid on the town in 1377 and another which set the town on fire in 1404, all part of the skirmishes with the French, with whom one king after another seemed to have a quarrel, life went on. Most lives were short and hard but trade from the port was carried on with Brittany (whose inhabitants spoke a very similar language), Ireland and France. As the tin trade prospered, so the port became busier. According to customs returns for 1205, Truro, Saltash and Lostwithiel were all suitable to carry on foreign commerce and Truro had jurisdiction over the whole river except what is now the inner harbour at Falmouth and the Penryn River. In the thirteenth century, when the Bishop of Exeter founded Penryn, Truro had supremacy over the whole river but, with the tendency of the river to silt up, Truro's power over it would wane in favour of Penryn. In just the same way, Tregony, a town upriver from Truro with a quay at the end of the street and sea traffic to make it prosperous ceased to be so when Truro took its trade. Falmouth at this time was spoken of in a little rhyme in derogatory terms, 'Truro was a thriving town when Falmouth was a furzy down', although the same rhyme has also been quoted as, 'Penryn was a thriving town when Falmouth was a furzy down'. Whichever it was, Falmouth was not highly rated at this time.

In 1413 the justices held an inquest to discover if the borough was so decayed that the taxes demanded could not be paid. The borough was once more in a sorry state, and by 1439 it was noticeable that many foreigners lived in the town. There were many Irish and also Scots, Breton, French and Dutch living and working here all of whom were taxed at a higher rate than the local population.

By 1497 the tinners were discontented. Henry VII was on the throne at this time and he exacted high taxes to fund his war with the Scots. Hard-pressed tinners were not interested in a war, especially as it was in such a remote place, and resistance built up throughout the county. In St Keverne the rumblings grew into revolt and under the leadership of Michael Joseph, the blacksmith, a group of men set off for London to tell the king personally how they felt. In Bodmin, Thomas Flamank, an eminent lawyer, was also expressing his disgust at the taxes levied and they joined forces with the men of St Keverne and others. No doubt some Truronians fell in with the group as they marched through town but seemingly no one of note as the names of those who went are not known.

On 16 June they reached Blackheath but instead of talking to the king and airing their views, they found themselves surrounded by the king's army. Some had already deserted but those who were left found that they were embroiled in a battle. The king's army, ready to advance to Scotland, were well armed and trained and the unwitting Cornishmen fought bravely with whatever they had. They were no match for the king's men, however, and Michael Joseph was captured and paraded through the city dressed in the kings colours of white and green. It is reported that he spoke as bravely as if he were at liberty but he was sent to the tower along with Thomas Flamank who was also captured. On 27 June they were both dragged from the tower on hurdles and taken to Tyburn where they were hanged, disembowelled and quartered.

Resentment increased among the Cornish, they were hard times indeed. By 7 September many of them rallied to the side of Perkin

Members of Truro Old Cornwall Society ready to welcome the marchers from St Keverne to Blackheath in 1997. From left to right, front row: J. Arnold Hodge, Betty May, Joyce Foster, Clarice Mortensen-Fowler, Margaret Mitchell and Peter Parnell with the banner.

Warbeck who claimed to be the younger of the two princes in the tower. He landed near Lands End, left his wife with the monks on St Michael's Mount and crossed the Tamar with about 6,000 men. They gained entry into the fortified city of Exeter but were eventually repulsed and so made their way to Taunton. It was here that Perkin Warbeck's courage failed him and he deserted the Cornishmen who had done so much for him. It took a lot of courage for the Cornishmen to leave their homes, livelihood and families and cross the Tamar and they had risked much for this imposter. The Cornish sadly made their way home and the king crushed them even more by extracting huge fines as a punishment for rebellion.

The events of 1497 made such an impression that 500 years later the first march to Blackheath was recreated. On this occasion the marchers were welcomed everywhere especially in London but in Truro they were greeted by the Mayor, councillors and civic dignitaries. The Truro Old Cornwall Society were also there to meet them at the top of Lemon Street and lead them down into the town with the society's banner flying. They were welcomed outside the cathedral and given refreshment before continuing on their way to London.

Although the fines for the county in 1497 came to over £600 and the people were struggling to pay, gradually things improved once more. Instead of just panning for tin the tinners became miners, digging for it. As mining fortunes improved, so did the coinage and the economy of

St Mary's Parish church from the east.

St Mary's Church from the East.

Truro. By 1504 a new church of St Mary was being built with permission to quarry as much stone as was needed from Sir John Arundell's manor, Truro Vean.

The port was as busy as ever and merchants were doing well in shipping. Thomas Tregian made a fortune and by 1530 his children were considered to be the best marriage matches in the county. In order to make money he was obviously very aware of the situation in the rest of the country. It is recorded that together with James Drew he broke a contract with a merchant in London. They were to buy iron and salt from him and send him tin but after the contract was made, the price of salt went down dramatically in Cornwall, so they refused to receive it or send him his tin.

The river, the highway to the sea, also caused problems with uninvited guests. A skirmish occurred in the Truro River between the French and the Spanish. The French had come almost as far up the river as Truro and then their flagship ran aground. They were definitely coming off worse in the encounter but the Spanish continued to attack them and refused to stop even when commanded to by Sir John Arundell. Both the French and the Spanish were hauled up before the justices of the peace in Truro who eventually allowed the Spanish to go first, followed later by the French. It was no wonder that the king was asked if blockhouses could be built down river to protect the towns inland from suffering this sort of nuisance.

By 1538 and with Henry VIII on the throne of England, the Dissolution of the Monasteries was in full swing. He had passed an Act of Parliament in 1536 which condemed many monasteries with incomes under £200. Due to protests in the north of England there was a delay in the Dissolution but after the Pilgrimage of Grace the rebellion was quashed and the Dissolution continued. After the monasteries it was the turn of the friaries and Truro surrendered their house two days after the Franciscans of Bodmin surrendered theirs. John Reskarnan and John de Coloribus together with nine other friars handed over the Dominican friary to the king. Title deeds that they held in safe keeping were handed to the Mayor as were furnishings, altars, books, etc. Many things were sold to meet the debts of £16 13s 4d and the site of the Blackfriars was bought by two gentlemen from Warwickshire. The buildings soon disappeared, probably much of the stone being taken to use in other constructions and today just the name of St Dominic Street remains.

So at the beginning of the sixteenth century changes were taking place in the old borough. The new church was being built, the friary was being demolished and another new establishment was founded. 1547 saw the beginning of Truro Grammar School founded by Walter Borlase. It was to last for many years and educate many boys who later achieved fame and fortune.

TRURO GRAMMAR SCHOOL 1881

After a pencil sketch by H. Michell Whitley

Truro Grammar School, 1881.

CHAPTER 4
The Seventeenth Century and the Civil War

During the years 1534-42 the king's librarian, John Leyland, undertook a tour of England intending to compile a survey of the whole country. Unfortunately he died before he could complete it but his notes still survive. He entered Cornwall over the New Bridge at Launceston in 1538 and travelled on to Tintagel Castle, Wadebridge, Padstow and Bodmin. He then went to the west of the county by way of Mitchell to St Ives, St Buryan, Godolphin and Helston, giving excellent descriptions of all the places he visited. He particularly liked rivers and after Falmouth he made his way up the river to Truro where he reported that the castle was 'clene down' and the area was used as a 'shoting and playing place'. 'Shoting' was archery practice and 'playing' in this case meant quarter-staff and cudgel play, compulsory games at one time, as these skills could be useful in defending the realm, although Ashley Rowe suggests that playing place meant that plays were still performed there. Perhaps it was with relief that Leyland later crossed back to the English side of the Tamar as his writings suggest that he was not too happy in Cornwall's wild and rugged parts but preferred the softer, wooded country of the south-east of the county.

It was not long after this that another change took place, not in the antiquities and historic sites that interested Leyland but one which was partly responsible for the loss of the Cornish language. The new English prayer book caused great unrest in both Cornwall and Devon. People had been accustomed to hearing their masses in Latin and enjoying regular performances of the old miracle plays in Cornish. In 1549 the Prayerbook Rebellion took place and although Truro seems to have mostly avoided being caught up in the trouble, both the mayor of Bodmin and the portreeve of St Ives were hanged.

By the second half of the sixteenth century things had settled down again and Truro was prospering. Instead of most of the coinage in the county being dealt with in Lostwithiel and Bodmin, Truro and Helston became the busier coinage towns with Truro even having a riot at the Coinagehall. William Godolphin had been appointed comptroller of the stanneries by Henry VIII but when Mary came to the throne she gave the job to a man called William Isham. On 4 July 1554 armed rioters forced their way into the coinagehall and demanded that Isham should leave and not meddle in Godolphin's affairs. William Isham, however, was not to be intimidated and he demanded the return of the coinage hammer from one of the men who had grabbed it, but he would not give it up. At this point William Isham was set upon and the Mayor was sent for but he refused to come, declaring that it was none of his business.

With the accession of Elizabeth I in 1558 the country which had been encouraged to follow the Roman Catholic religion under her sister Mary was now Protestant again. This was the time when many of the Catholic gentry took Jesuit priests into their homes in the guise of servants so they could continue with the religion of their choice. Many of these homes had 'priest holes' where the priests could be hidden in times of danger and they can still be seen in many stately homes today. Thomas Tregian, who had owned the ship Jesus and had married the heiress of Wolvedons (which brought him Golden Manor) had a grandson called Francis who took a Jesuit priest called Cuthbert Mayne into his house in 1575. Mayne had been born near Barnstaple and after his training as a Jesuit went to Golden and to all outward appearances was Francis Tregian's steward. For a couple of years Cuthbert Mayne was able to act as a priest for the Tregian family and other local gentry but it did not go unnoticed. In 1577 Richard Grenville, the sheriff, marched both Tregian and Mayne into Truro under arrest. Francis Tregian was imprisoned in London and his heavily pregnant wife, Mary Arundell, was turned out of her house with her three children in the dead of night. She was a courageous lady and set

Golden Manor.

off for London immediately only stopping on the way to give birth. She set about helping her husband who was eventually exiled to Portugal and is buried in Lisbon Cathedal. Cuthbert Mayne however, suffered a far worse fate as he was hanged at Launceston gaol and pieces of his body delivered to Tregony, Bodmin, Wadebridge and his home area of Barnstaple as a warning to any others who continued in the Roman catholic faith. Today his skull is a sacred relic at the convent at Lanherne.

It was in 1576, a year before their arrest, that Richard Grenville took over as sherrif. He was more of a seafaring man than a man who enjoyed life ashore. His friends were people like the Killigrews, Raleigh and Hawkins and he was an adventurer and privateer. Because Arundell and Tregian were anti piracy he did not get along with them and that was partly why he decided to use his new position to enquire into the situation at Golden Manor which led to the exile of Tregian and the death of Mayne. However, with the ever present threat from the Spanish, Grenville had men under his command who were armed and prepared to fight in the event of an invasion. In 1588 the Spanish Armada was approaching our shores and the fleet was sighted off the Lizard but worries that the ships might enter the Fal came to nothing. There must have been rejoicing when the fleet disappeared up the coast and never returned.

Another traveller gives us a brief picture of Truro during this time of the reign of Elizabeth I. In 1584 Norden wrote that it was 'a pretty compacted towne well peopled and wealthye marchauntes'. Only five years later Truro had a new charter from Elizabeth I confirming that it was a free borough with a Mayor and twenty-four Capital Burgesses. Four Aldermen were to be elected from the twenty-four, and there are still echoes of that today as the mayor is one of twenty-four councillors. In those days they had the right to elect the two members of parliament who served the town and to nominate a recorder, a steward of the court, two sergeants at mace and a coroner. The charter allowed no one to open a shop without the permission of the mayor although food could be sold at fairs and markets. It was now possible to have markets on Wednesdays as well as Saturdays as long as it did not upset any other towns nearby. Wednesday as market day continues today and for Truronians it was also 'pasty day' a convenient meal for people on busy days. The charter also mentioned the fact that Truro was an important coinage town and port and exhorted the people to keep the river from silting up.

The success of the port brought many merchants wealth and prominence and of course the new mayor and burgesses were also people of substance. The Mi[t]chell family held two of the council seats, John was the steward of the council and Hugh a capital burgess. Peter of the same family had sailed with Drake when he circumnavigated the world. Another family that made a fortune was the Robartes family. John married into the Gaverigan family and this is possibly how the site of his great house came into his possession. He made his money from timber and by lending money to the adventurers who invested in mines. Their house was three stories high and very long, extending from Boscawen Street for much of the length of King Street (names not in use in those days) on the site of the HSBC bank. Unfortunately this building is now gone but parts of it survived until the 1960s when the bank and Littlewoods were extended and Mr Douch, then curator of the museum, saved some door jambs. In 1620, Richard Robartes, son of John, bought Lanhydrock near Bodmin and set about building a grand house there.

Although the Robartes family were probably the most influential people in Truro there were other families of note. The Arundells of Lanherne owned land in the manor of Truro Vean and the Arundells of Trerice owned the manor of Allet. The Michell family were wealthy and owned land and had friends such as Francis Godolphin and Hugh Boscawen, who was himself busy acquiring land in Truro.

Other characters worthy of mention include Jenkin Daniell, a draper and the mayor of Truro in 1615. He erected the stone tablet in the market

The stone tablet from the old Market House, now in the Municipal Buildings.

IN
MEMORY
&HONOUR
OF THE LATE
Mr HENRY WILLIAMS
DRAPER OF THIS CITY
THE FOUNDER AND
BENEFACTOR OF THIS
CHARITY A·D 1631

house which was taken down when the old Market House was demolished and is inside the front entrance of the Municipal Buildings today. The inscription carved on it reads 'Who seks to find eternal tresure must use no guile in weight or measure' and is signed 'Ienkin Daniell, Maior. Another person whose name lives on today was another draper, Henry Williams. He made his fortune out of wool and has gone down in history as a likeable character who wanted to do good for his fellow men and his beloved town. Some people thought he was mad, as in 1623 he gave land to the borough so that it would have a better income! He also endowed a hospital, later known as the almshouses, and in1631 opened homes for ten poor people. He did the job properly and also provided a meadow so they could keep a cow and he gave property to endow the hospital. Among many other things, he remembered all his godchildren in his will (and there were many, as because he was known as a generous man everyone wanted him as a godfather for their children). He also left instructions in his will that a dinner should be provided for all his friends. He even thought to include the scribe who wrote out his long will for him. A neighbour of his, Francis Gregor, and his servant, John Greenwill, were accused by a Geo. Braye in a letter to three of Cornwall's most influential men – Sir William Killigrew, Francis Godolphin and Francis Basset – of forcing the elderly Henry to take a new wife and make a new will so that they could benefit from his property. Not only that but the letter suggested that they kept him 'close shut up' and declared him a lunatic. The receivers of the letter were asked to find out the truth and remove Mr Williams to safety. Poor Henry, he comes down the years as a kind and gentle man who died in1629 but still has a monument in the town he loved. The old almshouses have been knocked down but the bungalows which replaced them now stand on the opposite side of the road and provide cosy homes for those who benefit from his charity.

At one time Truro had another almshouse. A house was left to the poor of Truro by German Greer but with the advent of the railway this five-roomed house, divided into two, was sold because it stood on land required for the railway. The occupants were paid to move.

Another Truro character to appear in these days was Owen Phippen who was captured by Turkish pirates in 1620. He fought for his freedom a few years later with ten other captives and, overcoming their captors, he sailed the ship to port and returned home a wealthy man. As the brother of the rector of Truro he is commemorated by a plaque in the cathedral.

John White was also a benefactor to the town and he had thought about the future of the many orphans in Truro. People died younger than today and consequently many children were left with one or no parents. Born in Truro, John became a merchant in London and left money for the orphans to be apprenticed. Their apprenticeship lasted for approximately

Opposite: Monument to Henry Williams which stood in the grounds of the old almshouses in Pydar Street, now erected at Kestle Mill having been demolished with the buildings and found years later amongst some rubble at Newquay.

seven years during which time they were trained, fed and clothed. For the very poor the Poor Law relief from the parish was a form of help but was not so easy to obtain. The poor had to prove their place of residence to be eligible and disputes often arose between parishes.

During the 1620s Truro was in danger from pirates and the country was at war with at first Spain and then France. In 1626 Truro refused to let men attend the general muster and even as far back as 1619, the year before Owen Phippen was taken by the pirates, the mayor, Gregory Friggens, wrote a very 'loving' letter to Plymouth refusing to pay ship money towards the defence of the county. In 1640 Turkish ships were spotted off The Lizard but worse was still to come. Civil war was to break about the heads of the leading families in the county, forcing them to take sides, King or Parliament, and changing life for most people.

In 1642 Charles I found himself at odds with Parliament and on 22 August the Civil War began. It was not immediately obvious which side Truro would favour. The mayor, Jacob Daniell, son of Jenkin Daniell of the stone tablet, favoured Parliament but mayor choosing was imminent and Sir Richard Vyvyan so impressed the people of Truro with his speech outside the Market House that they decided for the king. The new mayor, John Michell, was also a Royalist. Sir Ralph Hopton had come to Truro during that year with his troops and also one of the most popular men in Cornwall, Sir Bevil Grenville of Stowe with Sir John Berkeley. It was Sir Bevil who inspired many willing Cornishmen, as in their minds they were fighting for him rather than some king who was somewhat remote.

The first battle in Cornwall probably had Truro men in the Royalist army. It was fought on Cornish soil in January 1643 at Braddock Down under the command of Sir Bevil Grenville. A few months later the battle was between the Cornishmen, again under Grenville and the parliamentary army of Devon under Lord Stamford. This was another victory for the Royalists with only half as many men as their opponents. Among the captured baggage of the parliamentarians was a large sum of money, £5,000. Francis Bassett of Tehidy wrote to his wife in jubilation two days later from Truro:

> Dearest Soule, Oh Deare Soule, prayes God everlastingly. Reede ye enclosed. Ring out yor Bells. Rayse Bonefyers, publish these Joyfull Tydings. Beleeve these Truthes. Excuse my writing larger. I have not tyme. We march on to meete our Victoryous ffrinds...

Things were going well for the Royalists in Cornwall. By July 1643 the Cornish had worked their way as far up-country as Bath and won another victory at Lansdowne but with disastrous consequences. Sir Bevil was mortally wounded and the story goes that his servant Anthony Payne, the

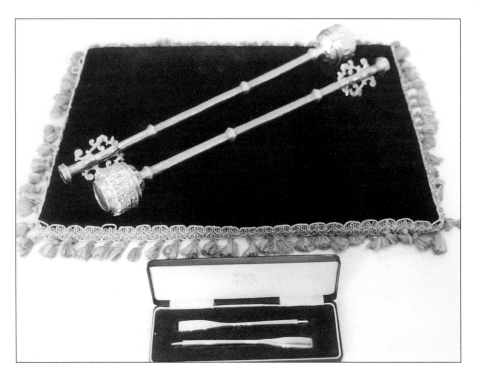

Cornish Giant, who stood seven feet four in his stockinged feet, lifted Sir Bevil's son John onto his father's horse. 'A Grenville, a Grenville' went up the cry from the Cornish who were fighting more for their beloved Sir Bevil than for the king and the ridge was taken and the battle won. Sir Bevil died the next day.

Another Grenville, but a completely different character from his elder brother, rode into Truro in 1644. Sir Richard had previously fought in Germany and Ireland and on his arrival back in England he was given money and troops by Parliament who expected him to fight for them. However, he had other ideas and rode off to Oxford to join the king. In 1644 he retreated to Truro after a battle in Lostwithiel where he tried to repulse Lord Essex who believed the Cornish were ready to capitulate. This was the information given to him by Lord Robartes, a strong parliamentarian whose home, Lanhydrock, was in Royalist hands. The Cornish were not ready to give in but the war was degenerating. They had lost many of their much-loved leaders and were poor, hungry and disillusioned. The rhyme 'The four wheels of Charles's wain – Grenville, Godolphin, Trevanion, Slanning slain' showed how important the Cornish were to the king's cause and how the county mourned their passing. The king thought especially kindly of his Cornish soldiers – if the poorly-armed rabble could be called that – and to this day a copy of his letter to them can be seen in many churches. Many of them were servants of his on Duchy land and in 1645 he appointed the Prince of Wales, Duke

The silver maces from the city regalia and the silver oars which are presented to each incoming mayor as a symbol of authority over the river.

35

of Cornwall, as commander of the western army and fifteen-year-old Charles came to Truro for part of the autumn and winter. By this time the Cornish were being taxed more than they could stand. At the outbreak of war the right to have first option to buy the tin from the mines had been granted to the queen, Henrietta Maria, and the proceeds used to buy weapons and ammunition, but now the mines were flooded and ill-tended. Harvests were lost, people were struggling with little or no money and many of the soldiers were undisciplined. By March 1646 Truro was ready for peace and the Royalists surrendered to Sir Thomas Fairfax, the Parliamentary commander. On 12 March 1646 the Treaty of Truro was signed on Tresillian Bridge and Hopton surrendered to Fairfax.

Although peace had come to Truro, further down the river at Pendennis Castle, Sir John Arundell of Trerice held out for another six months before marching out of the garrison, starved but with banners flying and trumpets and drums sounding.

For Truro there was brief period of fame as the home of the royal mint. Plate was brought from all over the county to be melted down and used for the king. Jonathan Rashleigh of Menabilly encouraged some of his more reluctant neighbours to part with their plate by giving them security in his own name. This proved rather costly as he later had to pay out £600. An entry in the records at the Custom House at Fowey states 'Item for charges of horse and men to carry a truncke of Lord Roberts his plate to Trewrow to the Mynt from Liskeard'. Lord Robartes, a Parliamentarian, evidently had some of his valuables 'released' after the Royalists won the battle at Braddock Down and his home was in Royalist hands. Mary Coate in her book 'Cornwall in the Great Civil War' tells of a half crown with particularly fine engraving depicting Charles I and dated 1642 which she believes was minted in Truro. A similar coin dated 1644 is believed to be a copy of the first and was minted in Exeter after the mint was moved there in 1643 when the town was once more in Royalist hands. The men who were deputed to find the workmen needed for the mint in Truro were, Mark Dethliffe of Gwennap, David Hawes of Redruth and John Rogers of Godolphin.

In 1642 the only goldsmith in Truro was John Parnell who had premises in the area of what is now Lower Lemon Street. His land would have stretched right back to the river and it was probably here that the mint was set up and the Royalist gentry brought their plate to be melted down for the king's cause. He was believed to have been the mayor at some time during the Civil War and to have been the maker of the maces still used today by the sergeants at arms. It was only in fairly recent years that the mark of John Parnell was recognised. Previously it had been thought to be the mark of Barnstaple but Mr Taprell Dorling recognised the ship of Truro (as on the arms of the city) and many items previously

thought to have been crafted in Barnstaple were recognised as having been from Truro.

Market Street and Fore Street with Middle Row between them still formed the business area of the town. Robartes used his 'great house' as a town house until the latter part of the century, we know it was still being used in 1658 but it was taken over by a family called Vincent a few years later. Another 'great house' was built by John Foote who acquired the land for it in 1682. In later years it was known and loved as The Red Lion.

Not everyone who owned a house was able to pass it on to the next generation in its entirety. In 1622 a lady called Christabel Michell provided for her family by leaving her property in King Street (probably where Etam now is) to all her children by giving them a few rooms each. At the other end of the century a Nicholas Sanders leased a house in King Street which gave him the right to place 'standings' in front of it, useful for selling things on market days. He also had the right to use an opeway to the river, and use of a meadow and an orchard. Truro still has several opeways – narrow passages connecting one street with another – Squeeze Guts Alley connects Boscawen Street and St Mary's Street, as does Pearson's Ope. Many of these opeways used to connect the town with the river, as Roberts Ope still does today.

The picture we receive is of a bustling market town with plenty of shops and commerce. Truro had an apothecary, a weaver, pewterers, drapers, a goldsmith, food outlets and many inns. Middle Row with the

market house was its heart with a cooper, a saddler and a barker. Truro continued to thrive, despite setbacks such as the civil war. Yet in the autumn of 1698, Celia Fiennes – travelling through Cornwall the only way to do it in those times, on horseback, and staying at Tregothnan with her cousin Hugh Boscawen – referred to Truro as formerly 'a great tradeing town, now a ruinated and disregarded place'. Although getting back to some sort of stability after difficult times this intrepid lady saw perhaps in Truro a faded elegance and a town which had fallen on hard times.

CHAPTER 5

The Eighteenth Century and some of Truro's outstanding characters

The eighteenth century did not start well. There had been wars in Europe which had caused a depression throughout the country and influenced the price and output of tin to levels much lower than before. There had been several disastrous harvests and crops had failed. The people were poor and hungry and the year 1700 saw food riots in Truro. As time went on the fortunes of the town did not improve; Falmouth was expanding as a port and taking trade from Truro. By 1709 the burgesses had to accept the fact that the boundary of the borough had shrunk considerably and instead of Black Rock forming the edge of Truro's jurisdiction over the river, it now stopped at Messack Point and Pencarrow Point.

In 1724 Truro had a famous visitor, the author Daniel Defoe who gave his opinion that Truro would never recover with Falmouth and its trade at the mouth of the river, fortunately, he was wrong.

The mining industry, always fluctuating, was soon improving and providing work again. Robert Lydall had been smelting at Newham using a new process involving coal rather than the much more expensive charcoal. Coal could be obtained relatively cheaply from south Wales and soon Lydall was ready to move to new premises. In 1711 Calenick smelting works opened for business, still using coal and not charcoal. Whether it was hoped that the new system would be a secret is not known but new inventions and modern technology have a habit of soon becoming known to all and when Samuel Enys and his business partner Henry Gregor built their new smelting works further up the valley in Treyew, they also employed the coal method of smelting. Samuel Enys prospered and gave Truro a beautiful building now known as the Old Mansion House which backed on to its own quay, still known today as Enys Quay. Originally a brick fronted building it is now plastered and although lack of maintenance placed it in grave danger a few years ago, it is well looked after now.

Enys was not the only man to prosper as a result of the upturn in mining. William Lemon rose from nothing to be universally known as 'The Great Mr Lemon'. Son of a poor man of Germoe near Helston, he found employment with John Coster, the inventor of the horse whim. Coster had come down from the Forest of Dean and before long William Lemon became his partner and a mine manager. In 1720 he was instrumental in bringing Thomas Newcomen to Cornwall and used

Calenick.

his steam driven beam engine to pump water from Wheal Fortune in the parish of St Hilary. This was a success and the first time that one of Newcomen's engines was used in Cornwall. In 1724 he married Isabella Vibert who brought him money that he invested in Wheal Fortune and so made his own fortune. He moved to Truro where he employed the architect Thomas Edwards to design and build a house for his family. It was situated opposite the coinagehall and is still there today. As Mr Lemon was a religious man it even had its own chapel, fitted out with an organ. Princes House was built around 1740 and the Lemons entertained on a grand scale. Out went the pewter tableware and only the best new china graced their table. Apparently the done thing was to drink down the tea then hold the delicate cup up to the light to admire it. One of the things that William Lemon had the courage to do was to study under the headmaster of the grammar school to make up for the education he lacked in earlier life. Although Princes House was new, stylish and ideal as a town house for winter where any pleasures that occurred in Truro could be enjoyed easily, Mr Lemon employed Thomas Edwards again to design a country mansion for him at Carclew. There was already a house on the site which was being built for Samuel Kempe who had married into the Bonython family but he had died before it could be completed so his widow sold it to William Lemon. Thomas Edwards was engaged and the house was enlarged and colonnades added and it became their country seat until it burned

The Old Mansion House.

Princes House.

down in 1934. This man who was made a capital burgess and was twice mayor of Truro died in 1760.

The master of the grammar school under whom Mr Lemon studied was George Conon, a Scotsman who held the post of headmaster from his appointment in 1729 until he resigned it in1771. He was known as a man of character and ability and the boys of Truro Grammar School could hold their own with any other school in the country. It is generally believed that the grammar school began in 1549 and was formed under Walter Borlase with the most likely place where lessons were held being the south porch of the parish church. The building known today as the old grammar school in St Marys Street is very close to that location but was part of the purpose built school which was in use from 1730. During the eighteenth century it had many pupils, some of whom became famous. Conon was famed for getting the number of pupils up from a handful to ninety nine at one stage but it was the joke of the town that he could never quite reach the hundred! He was a strong disciplinarian and would not hesitate to flog a boy who had flouted the rules or played truant.

The school was renowned for teaching classics but, although plays were studied, Conan really disliked the reading and acting of them. It was therefore rather unfortunate for him that one of his pupils went on to be the well-known and respected actor and dramatist Samuel Foote. He was born at Johnson Vivian's house (mayor of Truro 1741 and 1754) near the coinagehall on the site of the old Kings Head, roughly where Boscawen Street and Lower Lemon Street meet today. At one time a nunnery stood here and the nuns were known as Poor Clares. Their dwelling was known as Anhell or the hall. In 1741 he was entered for studies at the Inner Temple and actually studied law for three years. However it was the stage that drew him and he made his debut as Othello in 1744. He was described by a Dr Barrowby who met him socially, thus: 'One evening I saw a young man extravagantly dressed out in a frock suit of green and silver lace, bag wig, sword bouquet and point ruffles enter the room.' This was Foote who was known to be of a good family and a student at the Inner Temple at the time. He seemed well liked and he got on with most people but he did not like Garrick. He was a great success as a writer of satirical plays and as a comic actor and made himself a tidy fortune to add to his inherited money. Unfortunately he had no idea of how to look after it and spent his money freely. At one time he was in a debtor's prison in London when he received a letter from his mother telling him that she was in prison for debt and asking for him to come and help. He wrote back saying that he was also in prison for the same reason but as a dutiful son he sent his attorney down to help her! He used to like to visit his old school when in town but had a habit of giving the boys a day off without the master's permission which went down well with the pupils but not the

Boscawen Street, c. 1900.

staff. As soon as Foote made a name for himself on the stage, Conan took plays off the school curriculum! Samuel Foote died in 1777 at the Ship Inn in Dover on his way to France at the age of fifty-five and his epitaph read: 'Sacred to the memory of Samuel Foote Esq. who had a tear for a friend and a heart ever ready to relieve the distressed'.

The master who took over as head of the grammar school after George Conan was Cornelius Cardew, a man who came from Liskeard. The numbers had dwindled to only twenty-seven at the time he took over but during his incumbency, which lasted until 1805, it became very successful. Unfortunately in 1805 the numbers had shrunk again to only five pupils. Nevertheless during his time there, he had some pupils who were to become famous. Humphry Davy from Penzance was a pupil there for about a year in 1792. At the time the charge to attend the grammar school was £18 a year for board and £4 for the teaching received. After leaving the school in 1793, Davy was articled to Dr J.B. Borlase of Penzance. Best known for his invention of the miner's safety lamp, Davy was a brilliant scientist. Many school children have learned that 'Sir Humphry Davy lived in the odium of having discovered sodium' but another thing that many people should be thankful to him for was the discovery of the properties of nitrous oxide or ' laughing gas', something that he was working on when studying medicine in Bristol.

Another famous Cornishman to attend the grammar school was Henry Martyn. He was born in Truro in 1781 of 'humble parents' and sent to the grammar school at the age of seven. Cardew is reported by Ashley Rowe in his Chapters of the History of Truro to have described him as

Henry Martyn.

Henry Martyn
1781 – 1812

'frequently known to go up to his lesson with little or no preparation – as if he had learned it by intuition'. The lessons concerned were, of course, classics and this meek, studious young man – who was also described as 'of a lively cheerful temper' – did not go to Cambridge until 1797, having failed his exams in 1795. By 1802 he was a fellow and tutor at his college, St Johns. After a stay back in Truro at Woodbury he returned to Cambridge where he decided to become a missionary and was ordained at Ely in 1803. It was two years later that he started his studies in Hindustani and that same year he sailed for India where he started a church. During his life he translated the New Testament and the Book of Common Prayer into Hindustani and Persian but unfortunately he never lived to return home. He died in India in 1812 after an illness. He was aged just thirty-one.

Not all the pupils were so studious, but one, Edward Pellew was certainly brave. While a pupil at the grammar school he was rushing through the courtyard of the Red Lion one day to help put out a fire. On discovering that the back gate was shut he sprang over it in order to help. He would often play truant to go down to one of the many quays in town and look at the boats. After one of these jaunts he ran away to sea to avoid returning to an almost certain flogging from George Conan. In due course he became a captain in the Royal Navy and many Cornishmen, including miners who were struggling just to survive, served under him. He distinguished himself when a ship was wrecked off Plymouth in 1796 by swimming out to her through tremendous seas to get a line aboard. Many lives were saved (over five hundred) and Ned Pellew ended up with the title Viscount Exmouth for his trouble. A nickname by which he was known was 'Nelson of the navy's little ships'. Another local seafaring man also had a nickname, one which survives to this day, but he lived earlier in the century. Admiral Boscawen, member of parliament for Truro in the 1740s, was known as 'Old Dreadnought' and the playing fields at Hendra still glory in the name of Dreadnought Playing Fields.

It was not only the navy who benefitted from Truro's well-educated boys. Richard Hussey Vivian was sent to the grammar school when he was eight years old. In 1787 he went on to Harrow and joined the Regiment of Infantry in 1793. 1796 found him on garrison duty in Gibraltar. In 1809 his action saved many lives at Corunna and earned him the thanks of Sir John Moore. All this was leading to an even more dazzling victory when he played his part in the charge of the Light Brigade.

Although the men just mentioned were all pupils at the grammar school and it was acknowledged that education for women was far less

Dreadnought playing fields at Hendra.

A far cry from the meat dangling down and touching people's clothing at the old Market House, this window is magnificently dressed for a chamber of commerce competition. Nevertheless, it would be quite unacceptable under today's public health rules and regulations.

important, there were establishments for educating young ladies. One such was run by a Miss Mitchell, the daughter of the vicar of Veryan. It was never terribly successful as educational achievements were of less importance to young ladies than social abilities. Perhaps they might during some of their lessons read a little poetry, if so Andrew Brice might have been of interest to them, although he only stayed in Truro for a short time.

Andrew Brice of Exeter came to Truro and published a small book of poems called Poems on Several Occasions by Nicholas James. When he returned to Exeter in 1759 he produced The Grand Gazetteer which gave some very colourful descriptions of Truro. He described the old market house as a good one but was not impressed with the way meat hung down on long iron hooks so that it dangled against the clothes of people passing in the street, covering them with blood and grease. He also told of the country wenches standing like a row of soldiers with their baskets of geese, butter and poultry held before them. Of the town, he said:

'Tis a considerable Town with some regular Streets, well frequented Markets and a large Market-House. In very Deed (and all Joking laid aside) some modern Houses here, within as well as without, would not ill become the best Squares of London or of Westminster; nor might some of the best Inhabitants disgrace a Drawing-Room. In short, it is here as in most other Places: some Persons polite and genteel: some ill-bred and clumsy enough; some courteous, affable and good-natured; others supercilious, arrogant, morose, insolant; some whose Aspect and Demeanour look very engaging; others with Countenances quite dogged and forbidding; some fair-dealing; some cursedly tricking and rapacious.'

Later he goes on to say that the gentry are famed for politeness and hospitality: 'In Truth, very many live here so handsomely, and dress so very genteely, etc., etc., that the Pride of Truro and proud Truro are opprobrious bye-words among the Cornish'.

In 1754 the Truro Turnpike Company was formed and heralded a vast improvement in the state of the roads. In fact in 1775 Truro had another bridge to help traffic in and out of the town. This was the New Bridge, which still bears the name today, and crosses the River Allen further downstream from the Old Bridge. The gentry were able to travel in coaches rather than on horseback and families could be conveyed to entertainments in Truro to make the winter evenings more bearable.

New Bridge and Riverside Walk.

The toll house at the top
of Carvosa Road.

When Celia Fiennes came to Cornwall in 1698 even a lady of her standing had no option but to ride on horseback and the poor horse often stumbled into water-filled potholes on muddy roads. For many years the only coach in use in Cornwall was the Trewinnard coach, built in 1700 and used by the Hawkins family, reputedly for about eighty years! With the coming of the Turnpike Company came the toll-houses where the dues were to be paid. The cost of the toll for all the different classes of road traffic was posted up on boards and there was a stiff penalty for damaging any turnpike property.

It was not only the wealthy who were able to travel in more comfort and safety. In 1743 John Wesley paid his first visit to Cornwall and became lost in the 'great pathless moor beyond Launceston'. He found his way down through the county and preached to the poor overworked hungry miners who were eager for something better. Both John and his brother Charles were ordained members of the Church of England but soon Methodism was all the rage in Cornwall. It is amazing that with all the difficulties of travel he came to Cornwall more than thirty times. By the time he was eighty-six years old in 1789 he was able to travel in style. On arrival in Truro his carriage could not get to the preaching place for the mass of starving miners thronging the streets and the soldiers trying to subdue them. The miners were asking for a decent wage that they might live and when the carriage could go no further, Wesley alighted and preached outside the Coinagehall to far more people than could have squeezed into the preaching house.

In 1754 a Truro man, Thomas Daniell, a descendant of the Jenkin Daniell who had the stone tablet inscribed and set in the market house, married a lady called Elizabeth Eliot, a niece of 'the man of Bath', Ralph Allen. Thomas was already thirty-nine years old and had been in the employment of the Great Mr Lemon before becoming a businessman himself, so he was fairly well established. That and his wife's wealth placed him in a postition of prominence and soon he enhanced his status with a beautiful new house. The estimated cost of the house was £8,500. It was built in Princes Street and is known today as the Mansion House. The mellow gold stone with which it is faced came from Ralph Allen's quarries in Bath and was a handsome wedding gift. Thomas Daniell was not only a keen businessman but also a friendly man who liked to

Mansion House.

The Punchbowl and
Ladle at Penelewey.

entertain and was famous for his own blend of punch. Richard Polwhele, the Truro historian, told of the old gentleman who 'squeezed his lemons, flung in the sugar and the water and regularly gratified his company with a smack of the sherbet'. The rum was added later. Ashley Rowe suggests that the public house, The Punchbowl & Ladle at Penelewey, might be named as a compliment to Thomas Daniell, especially as it is bordered by land once owned by him.

The year after the marriage of Thomas and Elizabeth saw the birth in Truro of a boy called Henry Bone, the son of a carpenter. It is believed the carved wooden pulpit now in the cathedral was the work of the father, and the son went on to find fame as a painter of enamels and as portrait painter to members of the Royal Family. He was apprenticed to William Cookworthy and went with him to his porcelain works in Bristol where he was considered the best painter of porcelain. He later moved on to Randle & Company of Paternoster Row in London where he specialised in enamel painting, particularly on fans. Dr Wolcot realised what a talent he had and recommended annual painting tours of Cornwall. His first painting at the Royal Academy was that of his new wife Elizabeth. He became enamel painter to George III, George IV and William IV and died in December 1834. It was said of him that 'unaffected modesty, generosity, friendship and undeviating integrity adorned his private life.'

Another family of note in the town was that of the Rosewarnes. They were neighbours of the Lemons and Daniells, their house being where Oscar Blackford had his printing works for many years. Henry Rosewarne made much money out of smelting and built the smelting house at Carvedras. He was a capital burgess and a mayor of Truro but had ideas of becoming an MP and after much plotting on the council and ignoring the

wishes of Lord Falmouth who usually dictated his choice, Rosewarne was elected and Bamber Gascoyne re-elected. Henry was a friend of Pitt the Younger and not only used to visit him at Boconnoc but used to entertain him to dinner in his great house in Truro. However such a scandal had been created that it hit the national newspapers of the day and Pitt turned his back on Rosewarne. Henry died in 1783 after he had moved to his new house at Bosvigo.

Another person who had fallen out with the corporation was Dr John Wolcot, also known as Peter Pindar. Born in Devon, he sailed to Jamaica with Sir William Trelawny when he was going out to take up the post of Governor but returned to England when he had news that the incumbent of a rich living was dying. The obliging Bishop of London made him a deacon one day and ordained him a priest the next and he set off for Jamaica again only to find that the man had not died after all! He took a much poorer living but soon tired of it and returned to England to continue his other career, that of physician. He caused anxiety in the other doctors of the town as he had experience of a much wider variety of illnesses than they did but he was welcome everywhere at the social events as he was a good conversationalist. His patients thought highly of him for many reasons. He did not trust the apothecaries and when he had prescribed a medicine he examined it and sometimes detected that the apothecary had substituted a cheap medicine when a much more expensive one had been ordered. On one occasion he threw the pills prescribed for a patient by another of the town's doctors, Dr Warrick, out of the window! He certainly took the health of his patients very seriously and they loved him for it. For many years he lived in a house facing The Green and wrote satirical verses which amused everyone – except those

*Dr John Wolcot alias
Peter Pindar.*

" Peter Pindar "
Dr. John Wolcot 1738 – 1819

whom he satirised! At one time, when James Kempe was mayor, Wolcot was ordered by the overseer John Buckland to take an apprentice. Kempe and his father-in-law, Christopher Warrick, were the town's other physicians and there was no love lost between them and Wolcot. The latter, who steadfastly refused to take an apprentice, said that he was moving to Helston and they could put the apprentice through the keyhole, inferring that the poor children were starving. He went on to write a poem entitled 'The Hall' which began:

The Sages met in full Divan
To wreak dire vengeance on the man
Who to John Buckland wrote Epistle
Bidding the Alderman go whistle.

On one occasion Wolcot found himself in really hot water as James Ma'Carmick challenged him to a duel. James was born in 1742 and educated at the grammar school. He had served in the army and, after his retirement, became mayor of Truro in 1771. He later represented Truro as MP for three years, 1784-1787, and then seems to have continued his army career, as by 1813 he was a general. He was also one of Truro's wine

Penmount.

merchants for a time. In 1775 he bought an estate, Penhellick, but he tore down the house and built a new one, calling it Penmount. Wolcot had said something which he himself described as 'more severe than just' to the general which led to another caustic remark. The general at once issued a challenge to Wolcot to meet him on The Green at 6 a.m. the next day where the affair was to be settled with pistols. Wolcot's house looked out on to The Green and, as he was dressing the next day, a little before the appointed time, he looked out into the cold morning and saw the general pacing up and down. There were no seconds and Wolcot, who had spoken in the heat of the moment the night before, thought of an escape from the desperate situation he was in. In his own words as he told it to Cyrus Redding, which were then printed by Ashley Rowe in *Some Chapters in Truro History*:

I rang for my servant, ordered a fire to be instantly made, and breakfast and toast to be got ready. It yet wanted something of the time, and when the hour was up, I opened the door that looked upon the Green, crossed it with the aspect of a lion and went up to Ma'Carmick. He did not utter a syllable. "Good morning General" The General bowed stiffly. "This is too chilly a morning for fighting". "That is the alternative, sir, in case I have no other satisfaction." "What you soldiers call an apology, I suppose? My dear general, I would rather make twenty, when I was so much in the wrong as I was last night. I will apologise, but on one condition only." "I

Looking across the Kenwyn River to The Green.

cannot talk of conditions", said the general gravely, but evidently with less stiffness than before. "Why then I will consider the conditions accepted! They are that you will come in and take a hearty breakfast with me – it is ready."

So the two old friends shook hands and put the world to rights over breakfast. With no seconds present no one had lost face and no one else was any the wiser.

In 1781 Wolcot decided to leave Truro. He had probably fallen out with most of the town, having made them the butt of his jokes, but he had another motive as well. He had been encouraging a fifteen-year-old boy to develop his artistic talents. He had also been buying materials and putting opportunities in his way. He decided that the boy could prosper in London and, sure enough, John Opie became a successful artist. Under his pen name of Peter Pindar, John Wolcot became the most successful satirist of his day.

Also, in 1781, the old folks in the almshouses lost their hospital field for the cow as the burgesses decided to build the workhouse there. Other changes had taken place in the town. The new Byfield organ had been installed in St Marys, probably donated by Mr Lemon and in 1765 the corporation decided to build a new steeple for the church as the current one was described as 'a pitiful little thing – looking more like a Pidgeon-hut'. In 1770 Lord Falmouth gave the Great Bell at a cost of about £150. According to local historian Dr Taunton, before that, people were called to church by the ringing of a hand bell.

Part of the steeple of the old St Mary's parish church, erected at Diocesan House, Kenwyn.

The cross from the top of the steeple from St Mary's, some of the words inscribed round the base read: 'High over busy Truro town of Mary's church this topmost crown.'

The Assembly Rooms in High Cross.

It was in 1769 that Mr Edward Giddy announced in the Sherbourne Mercury that his hostelry The Red Lion would be closing but that he would be moving only two doors away to Mr Foote's Great House and re-opening there. Perhaps a few years later it was open for refreshment for people who had been to the new assembly rooms, built in High Cross. During the century High Cross was still the site of weekly markets and the fairs that came round each year. The bull-baiting still took place there with the bull tethered to an iron ring in the base of the cross but for more

The Royal Cornwall Infirmary, now closed.

genteel entertainment it was decided to build the new assembly rooms and the money to do so was raised by tontine. Lord Falmouth bought three shares at a cost of £55 each, with twenty-five other shares bought by different people. Each purchaser had to nominate a life. While that life survived the owner of the share had a say in the running of the building and enjoyed part of the profits, but when their nominated life died so did the subscribers interests. It opened in 1789 and Sarah Siddons, the famous actress, came to the ceremony. There were many glittering occasions at the assembly rooms with ladies and gentlemen elegantly dressed and soldiers in their uniforms. A Mr G.W. Maton, visiting the town in 1790, gave as his opinion that Truro was 'unquestionable the handsomest town in Cornwall'. The rich were getting richer, in fact Ralph Allen Daniell's nickname was 'Guinea a minute' as that was what he was believed to earn, but trouble was in store.

In 1793 the country was at war with France and in 1795 the harvest failed, followed the next year by another bad one. Landowners were becoming wary, afraid that the French Revolution would possibly give ideas to the lower classes here. However, there was an upturn in spirits in 1798 when Nelson defeated the French and a celebration ball was held, an elegant affair for the wealthy. Meanwhile, a new prison was built near the almshouses as most of Middle Row had been cleared away including the old prison next to the old coinagehall. In 1799 the new hospital which had first been discussed in 1790 by Sir Francis Basset was opened on the twelfth of August, the birthday of its patron, the Prince of Wales.

CHAPTER 6
An Adventurous Age

A man who was mourned by many died in Truro in the year 1800. His name was John Martyn and, together with his business partner, William Petherick, he leased a building at Truro Vean in which he set up a carpet factory. As Petherick was a dyer they also leased a building near the mill pool where the spinning jennies could be heard clattering away. Martyn employed many people who were disabled, either because they were born like it or because they had suffered an accident. They were people who would otherwise not be able to earn their own living. It is no wonder he was so highly regarded during times with no social security system. Perhaps one point that was not so forward-looking and correct was shown when a visitor to the manufactory wrote a description of the complete process from spinning to the actual weaving of the carpet. He stated that 'some of the shops have only women and girls to weave the inferior carpets and in other shops only men and boys to weave the cut carpets with large flowers'. Perhaps Mr Martyn had regard for the fact that most men had families to keep whereas the women, for the most part, did not.

Also in that year 'Guinea a minute Daniell' bought Trelissick overlooking the Fal and with a view up-river to Tregothnan, the residence of the Boscawen family. Changes were taking place in the town too. The King's Head was a popular inn recorded as having a panelled room with carved figures of apostles and an arched window which suggests that it could at one time have been a chapel for the guild of St Nicholas but it was removed to make a space for the new road, Lemon Street, to descend into the new wide Boscawen Street. Pearce's Hotel was built to replace it and beside the new hotel was the new bridge over the Kenwyn, to be known as Lemon Bridge where once stepping stones had forded the river. The Quicksilver coach would leave Falmouth each morning and reach Pearce's for lunch then on to Launceston for dinner and so to London, several days away. In 1846 Queen Victoria and Prince Albert moored the royal yacht in the Fal and Prince Albert came ashore to visit the town. Henry Pearce who entertained the prince changed the name of his hotel to The Royal in the prince's honour after being granted permission to do so. The terracotta coat of arms that he placed over the door was so badly damaged by fire in 1893 that it was removed but a new badge, beautifully painted, has been positioned over the door during recent

The Millpool.

years. Provisions for the hotel and horses came from two farms owned by the hotel, one of which, Royal Farm at Kenwyn, still retains its name.

Other building work went on apace in the town and much of it was due to the talent of an amazing man. Philip Sambell was born in Devonport in 1798, the son of a timber merchant who came to Truro to live in 1822 and settled in Fairmantle Street. Not only did he draw up plans for several streets including River Street, Castle Street and St Georges Road but also he designed many of Truro's beautiful buildings. St Marys Methodist Church, now known as Truro Methodist was built in 1830, the museum in River Street built as a savings bank in 1845 and the Baptist church, now part of the museum, begun in 1848, were all Sambell buildings. Although no-one is sure, Walsingham Place also could well be built to his

*The Royal, built as
Pearce's Hotel in 1800.*

*The entrance to Royal
Farm at Kenwyn.*

The Royal Cornwall Museum, built as a savings bank, and the former Baptist chapel.

design. Another of his architectural features is the column of the Lander monument and while working for Sir Charles Lemon he designed Strangways Terrace. All this was the more remarkable because he was born deaf and mute and yet was educated to such a standard that he was able to work as a successful architect. He also prepared papers which were read on his behalf to learned societies. He returned to Devonport and died in 1874 leaving a marvellous memorial in his many beautiful buildings.

However there were some structures that were definitely not of his design! Before the beginning of the century the militia was billeted in the town but in 1803 work started at the top of Lemon Street on the building of a barracks. Designed to accommodate 180 horses as well as the soldiers, the buildings were to be in two parallel lines overlooking the town. This would give a panoramic view of the town to those living there and the barracks themselves, plastered and stuccoed, would supposedly add to the elegance of the town. Intended to be completed in three months, people were optimistic about the early completion of the new addition to the town but the local paper reported four months after work started that the work was behind schedule due to a shortage of workmen. However in the following January a roof blew off and parts of the walls were blowing away showing how poorly the barracks were being constructed. By 1804 what had been planned as attractive wood buildings plastered over, were bare board and even when later they were tarred over they gave no protection to the inmates. In winter they were bitterly cold and during the flea season, the men preferred to sleep with their horses rather than be eaten alive. Perhaps it is just as well that today only the name Barrack Lane survives!

It was in the Gazette that the news broke upon Truro that it was to have a barracks. For many years the closest thing to a local newspaper was the *Sherborne Mercury* which never had news that was very local due to the large area it had to cover and an additional drawback was that by the time copies reached Truro, the news was several days old. In 1801 the first newspaper published in Cornwall made its debut. It was the *Cornwall Gazette & Falmouth Packet*. It only lasted just over a year then the owner Thomas Flindell moved to Truro and seized on the opportunity of publishing a paper as Harry Vivian had proposed setting up a paper for Truro but the historian Polwhele had hesitated. Polwhele wrote, 'but for my pusillanimous hesitation Harry and I should have come out as joint editors. On my declining the business Flindell seized upon the project and boldly stepped forth and carried it into execution'. Born down in the Helford at Manaccan in 1767 Flindell had already worked as a printer in Bath, London and as far away as Edinburgh but it was in Truro with a list of subscribers including the Prince of Wales that he came into his own. He set up a printing press in Lemon Street and on 2 July 1803, the *Royal Cornwall Gazette* was published. This local newspaper would have been in great demand with all the important events shortly to be announced. It was the first paper to publish news of Trafalgar and of Nelson's death, the news having been brought to town when a post chaise stopped at the Royal Hotel for just long enough to change horses.

Cyrus Redding, to whom John Wolcott gave his account of the duel that never was, was a newspaper man. He was born in Truro in 1785 and was a pupil of Truro Grammar School.

When the West Briton was launched in 1810 he was the only Truronian on the staff and he stayed in Truro to see that all went well, although he later moved to Plymouth and sent articles down for the paper. One such article was an account of the destruction of Nelson's old ship Captain during a great fire in the Hamoaze. The first issue of the West Briton was printed and published by a local printer, John Heard of 30 Boscawen Street. It was issued on 20 July 1810 at the cost of sixpence halfpenny.

Something else that would no doubt have been in the paper was the fact that Truro endured a scandal in 1812 but the dreadful details are all a bit vague. A man called James Stephens was a Methodist preacher and reports suggest that he preached to congregations of 'many thousands' at the site of the old castle. He then committed a 'shameful crime' and was thrown out of the Methodists, only to flee to King Harry Ferry where he drowned himself to escape arrest. He was buried on the castle site which caused local people to avoid it for many years to come.

In 1811 a meeting was held at Pearces Hotel consisting of members of the nobility, clergy and gentry with the aim of establishing schools to

Steam-driven version of the King Harry Ferry.

educate the children of the poor 'upon Dr Bell's System in the Principles of the Christian Religion as taught by the Established Church'. It was to be a countywide project but by April 1812 the Truro schoolroom was open for business with Mr Brenchley as the first master. It was known as the Cornwall Central School and was probably situated in the River Street/Tippet's Backlet area of town as we know that they were allowed to bring part of the higher leat through the premises. Boys to be educated were admitted free if they were from a poor family, or if the parents could pay, the charge was four shillings each quarter for lessons in reading. It was three shillings a quarter extra for the two extra subjects of writing and arithmetic. Before long the numbers of pupils were more than expected but truancy was frowned on even if the school was overcrowded. Richard Penliggan, Thomas Clark and John Sim were all dismissed and lost their places at school.

In 1814 the peace was celebrated in great style by the inhabitants of Truro. After twenty-one years of war with the French, people were ready to celebrate and on Monday 25 June an illumination of the town was to take place. The church bells were rung to signal the time for lighting and every window in the town had some form of illumination in it even if it was only a candle. One of the main highlights of the day was a procession of men dressed as Cossacks who went round the town. They were guarding a man who was supposed to be Napoleon. At midsummer they really went to town on the celebrations and there was a furry dance and an official dinner at the Red Lion. The town was bedecked with garlands raised high enough so that the mail coach could still get through. There was a square pavilion at each end of Middle Row (it still seems to have

been there although conflicting reports suggest it was demolished, probably it came down piecemeal) with a larger one in the centre near Lemon Street and long tables were laid out with plenty of roast beef, plum pudding and strong beer. It was enough to feed 1,000 people and later 1,600 children had tea and cake, quite possibly the large saffron buns still remembered today as the usual fare to be had on a Sunday School outing. There was public tea drinking at High Cross and a furry dance in which everyone joined regardless of class. It continued until late and the young carried on the celebrations the next day. Those peace celebrations were supposed to start on Thursday 23 June but people were impatient, so it was agreed that they would start on the Tuesday instead. However, a band of twenty young men started to parade round the town playing their music at midnight on the Monday and they kept it up until seven the next morning! It is a wonder that anyone was fit to start celebrating the next day!

Another great event to be reported in the papers with pride was the victory at the battle of Waterloo in which a Cornishman, General Sir Richard Hussey Vivian played an important part by leading the decisive cavalry charge. His parents home was where Truro Methodist Church is today and he received a hero's welcome after his distinguished service with the Duke of Wellington. The townsfolk went out to meet him and bring his carriage home to Truro, pulling it themselves. Later there were celebrations at the Assembly Rooms which was decorated with flags and garlands for the occasion and an excellent dinner was served. He later went on to be the MP for Windsor from 1825-30 and died far away from his native Cornwall in Baden Baden in 1842. He was remembered as 'An excellent officer and better still a kind, brave, honourable and good man.'

The Assembly Rooms rivalled those of Bath and for a brief spell Truro was just as elegant with the gentry of the county keeping town houses and enjoying the winter entertainments. One of the most popular musicians to play there in the early part of the century was Joseph Emidy who had been captured as a slave from the west-coast of Africa. Emidy was a talented musician who could not only compose music but also play the violin and teach the piano and flute among other instruments. It was in Lisbon that Captain Pellew first saw him perform and arranged for him to be captured once more so that Emidy could entertain on board Pellew's ship. Eventually, several years later Pellew gave Emidy his freedom and he settled in Truro, married the daughter of a tradesman and made his living playing his violin and performing in many concerts. He died in Truro in 1835 and is buried in Kenwyn churchyard. Perhaps he not only played his own music but that of other Truro composers. Giles Farnaby was born in Truro around 1564 and became famous in London with his madrigals and keyboard music and Francis Tregian of Golden Manor, before being exiled

Banner of Truro Old Cornwall Society, founded in 1922, showing part of the arms of the city.

The Red Lion Hotel.

The mayor, Councillor Mrs Myra Pryor and the town crier during Edwardian Week in 1995.

The Council Chamber with the bust of Dr Clement Carlyon behind the mayor's chair.

The outside of the cathedral baptistry, dedicated to Henry Martyn.

The Coinagehall, built as a bank on the site of the original coinagehall.

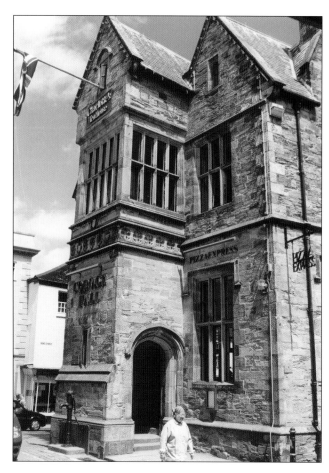

The Dean's office and Old Bridge Street.

Truro's War Memorial and the town clock above the Municipal Building.

The Hall for Cornwall.

Walsingham Place, much loved by John Betjeman.

The river at Truro beside Garras Wharf.

Trennick Mill Café at Boscawen Park, once known as The Junket House.

Dreadnought playing fields at Hendra.

The rear of Bishop Philpott's Library with a carved stone mitre above the window.

The doorway of the Royal Hotel with Royal coat of arms.

Downriver from New Bridge looking towards Furniss' Island.

Cathedral Lane, formerly called Church Lane and before that Street Edy.

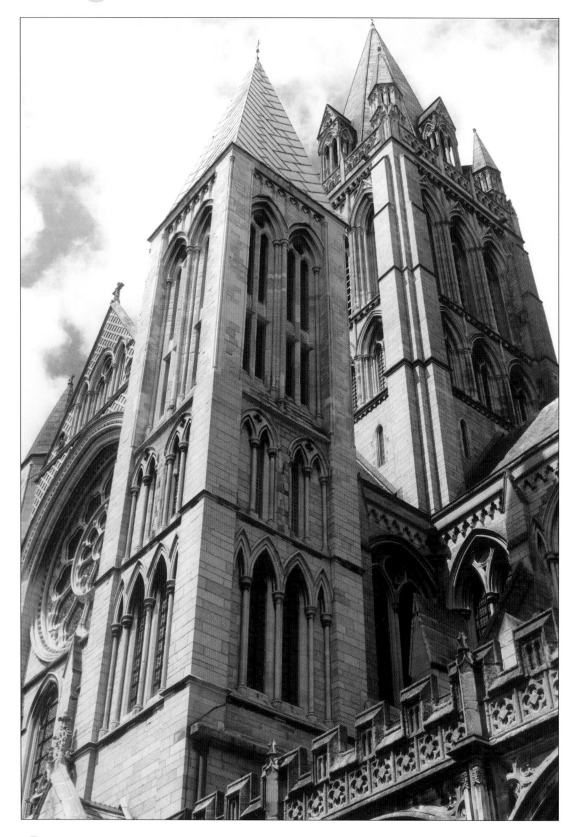

Opposite: *The cathedral clock tower coated in copper, the clock was removed when it became dangerous.*

Right: *The City Council's David Thomas in the Mayor's Parlour holding one of the maces.*

The top of Lemon Street. Barrack Lane is on the left behind the monument but the barracks, now demolished, were a failure from the moment they were built.

Looking down Chapel Hill with the old Roman Catholic Church on the left.

Sunny Corner, on the road to Malpas.

The museum in River Street. The section on the right was the Baptist chapel and the main section on the left was built as a bank.

St Paul's Church.

The Punchbowl & Ladle.

The modern version of Boscawen Bridge with the old lockgates.

The bandstand in Victoria Gardens.

*The fountain in Victoria Gardens, moved
from Boscawen Street in 1937.*

The new piazza with Truro School on the horizon.

High Cross.

*The Municipal
Buildings.*

to Portugal, whiled away his time in the Tower of London by compiling the Fitzwilliam Virginal Book.

It was on 4 June 1832 that the Reform Bill became law. Before then only the mayor and burgesses had the right to vote but now that right would be granted to many. Naturally the council resisted change and supported the old way along with the newspaper The Gazette but the new paper the West Briton was on the side of the reformers. When the act was passed there was much excitement and anticipation in Truro and people were awake and waiting for the 5 a.m. mail coach. The good news was relayed to the inhabitants that the reformers had won and the gun on Back Quay was fired. Flags appeared and the town took on a festive air. At noon there was a procession with the almost inevitable band and days of celebration followed. Tea drinking in Pydar Street had at least 1,000 elderly people enjoying tea and cakes and Truro was not the only town celebrating. At Grampound there was a feast and flora dance and the same at Falmouth with the addition of speeches. By 24 August everything in Truro was ready for a public dinner at half a crown a plate. The would-be diners marched through the decorated town to Mr Sambell's timber yard and enjoyed the meal cooked by Mr Pearce in his hotel.

Although politics had taken up a great part of peoples' time in the preceding years, it did not monopolise all their leisure time. In 1825 Truro

Tippet's Backlet before the old cottages were demolished.

Races began and after several weeks of advertising, on the 30 August there were three main events. The Subscription Cup valued at fifty sovereigns was a race open to non-thoroughbred horses. The next was a race for ponies, with a bridle and saddle as first prize and spurs as second. The third race was for 'horses, the bona fide property of NCOs and privates of yeomanry cavalry' with a silver cup for the winner. The next year the races were well advertised again but in 1827 they were rather overshadowed by a court case held in Bristol. Mr Stevens of the Red Lion had intended to give the stewards who dined with him turtle, amongst other delicacies, which he ordered from Mr Pring of Bristol. Eight quarts of turtle were duly despatched but never arrived at the Red Lion. However, there was more than enough turtle soup for those dining at Pearce's Hotel, in fact far more than was ordered!

A few years later in 1832 there was another spectacular entertainment for the people of Truro. Mr Sambell's timber yard was taken over for two days by a huge balloon which took those two days to fill with gas from the gasworks. Mr Graham was to make an ascent in the balloon which could rise four miles high, quite a sight. The gasworks had been one of the first in the country and by 1820 many of the streets had gas lighting. It certainly came in handy for filling the balloon although it did not travel far and came down at Polwhele.

Truro must have been a mixture of sights and smells in those days. For example, there was still a dung heap by the churchyard wall giving offence to all by its size and odour. Back in 1744, the rector had complained about it to the Bishop and Doctor Spry (born in St Clement Street in 1801, and later an avid collector of local anecdotes and a historian) was told that the three old men who were the scavengers had forty shillings each every year, a suit of clothes lined with yellow at Christmas and all the dung. They would sell it for one shilling a load and help to load it themselves. This dung heap was very near the Assembly Rooms where many events took place and the wealthy arrived bedecked in their finery and stepped from their coaches and carriages. Truro was fashionable and elegant but not yet very sanitary.

A new building was being erected in Boscawen Street to the design of Christopher Eales, the Italianate styled municipal Building. Now that Middle Row was gone this elegant building fronted the new wide thoroughfare and gave a suitable home to the mayor and burgesses. On the ground floor was the police station which housed the borough force and at one time the rear of the building housed the fire brigade's engine.

Another building, this time gracing the new development in River Street was the museum which was built as a savings bank in the 1840s. River Street looked very different in those days as the course of the river has been altered since. At the other side of town, Mr. Tweedy who had come to Truro to take charge of the Cornish Bank had a Friends Meeting house built. He and his wife were members of the Society of Friends and had the Quaker Meeting House erected in the corner of the garden of his house, Truro Vean (now Benson House). The famous Quaker Elizabeth Fry attended and spoke at the opening ceremony in 1825.

Truro had its share of interesting characters. Ann Hore was a lady blacksmith, a demanding job for a man, let alone a woman. Another woman in a man's world was Jenny Mopus and no book about Truro would be complete without a mention of her. She died in 1832 at the grand old age of eighty-two and spent her life working as a ferry woman at Malpas. When asked what gave her most trouble in her work, the reply had been

Entrance to the Quaker Meeting House.

Malpas ferry, c. 1900.

'Wemmen and pigs' although in fact she had foiled a troublemaker herself when she rescued Lord Falmouth's post in 1804. Although the post boy was overcome by the thief, he was no match for Jenny and the post was rescued and the thief sent to Bodmin goal.

John Nichols Tom was another colourful local character. His father was the landlord of a public house in St Columb and his mother gloried in the name of 'cracked' Charity. Perhaps this should have given people a clue as to his character as he had quite an eventful life. He was articled to a solicitor for a few years then became clerk to the Truro wine merchants, Plummer & Turner where eventually he took over the business. Not long after it became his in 1828 the premises burnt down and he left town in a hurry with the insurance money, causing tongues to wag. His destination was Liverpool, from whence he travelled abroad and then returned to Canterbury in 1832. H.L. Douch tells us in *The Book of Truro* that Tom posed as 'Count Rothschild, Sir William Percy Honeywood Courtenay, Knight of Malta and King of Jerusalem' and put up for a parliamentary election! Not surprisingly he spent some time in a lunatic asylum but in 1838 he appeared again believing himself to be the Messiah. Others believed him as well as he led a revolt of peasants from Kent, angry about the Poor Law, fought both police and army which lead to the deaths of two men and was then shot himself.

More respectable local notables were the brothers Richard and John Lander. The elder of the two was Richard who was given the second Christian name Lemon in honour of Colonel John Lemon, MP for Truro

Richard Lemon Lander.

Richard Lander 1804-1834

Statue of Richard Lander on its column. Carved by Cornish sculptor Nevill Northey Burnard and designed by Philip Sambell, it overlooks the city from the top of Lemon Street.

who was elected on the day Richard was born. The Lander family lived in what many Truronians today will remember as the Dolphin Inn which ended its days as a snack bar but was once known as the Fighting Cocks Inn. Richard attended a school in Coombs Lane known as Old Pascoes School and was a bright-eyed boy of below average height. Richard set off to seek his fortune in much the same way as Dick Whittington: he went to London at eleven years old and worked as a servant to a merchant who had the opportunity to travel and Richard accompanied him to the West Indies where he stayed for three years. He had a fever in St Domingo and returned to England in 1818. In 1823 he went to the Cape of Good Hope with Major Colebrook and returned home again in 1825. It was Africa that caught his imagination and that was where he went with his brother John and the backing of the government to try to discover the source of the Niger. They managed to untangle some of the obscurity surrounding the great river and its delta but on the third visit to the area Richard and his party were attacked by natives from Hyammah, an island about 100 miles from their destination at Fernando Po. Richard was encouraging his group who were fleeing in canoes when he was shot and wounded in the hip, a wound which subsequently killed him. He is buried on Fernando Po but is remembered in Truro by a fine monument.

In 1835 his young daughter led the procession to the top of Lemon Street where it was planned to have a memorial to him. It took longer than expected to complete as the original column, designed by Philip Sambell, collapsed and, according to Polwhele (who thankfully seemed to be everywhere in Truro, saw and heard everything and had the good sense to write it down) the crash shook all Lemon Street. When completed in 1852 and surmounted by a statue carved by Nevill Northey Burnard it was a monument to be proud of. The monument is still well looked after today although it needed some serious renovation in the last few years. By the time it was complete John had also died of a disease contracted on the expedition that he made, so quite rightly his name is recorded as well.

The status of Truro changed in 1838 with the abolition of the coinage but by this time the town was well established and not so dependent on such an old custom to bring trade and prosperity. In 1847 Lord Falmouth praised Dr Clement Carlyon for instigating changes in the public health of the town. Truro had escaped a cholera outbreak in 1832, something of a miracle as open sewers ran through the streets. However, extra scavengers had been taken on to keep the streets clean and water from the leats flowed through the gutters to keep the town clean and wash away the debris. Another danger, particularly in the summer months was the threat of rabies and dogs had to be muzzled, until in 1835 the first new council after the reform said that dogs not muzzled would be rounded up and destroyed and proceeded to carry out their threat.

The police force in Truro was born from a meeting in May 1822 when the mayor called the townspeople together to see if they could sort out the 'frequent occurrence of night broils in the street'. Action was deferred until after 1829 when Sir Robert Peel founded the Metropolitan Police. The Municipal Corporations Act of 1835 stated that the new corporations formed should raise a watch committee and Truro's

The Dolphin Buttery, formerly the Fighting Cocks Inn, now demolished in order to widen Green Street.

A float of the Welfare Centre from a carnival parade, around 1933, passes the entrance to today's Lemon Street market. The lady in black is Mrs Nicholls with her children Frances and Frank.

committee was based on the model of the Metropolitan Police using the five borough constables and an inspector to be taken from London. Consequently, in November 1839, Dunstan, Courties, Couch, Burnett and Lowry were sworn in to work under Inspector Paine. With the police station housed in the municipal building as well as the town hall which was used as a magistrates' court a common threat to miscreants was 'I'll have you under the clock'.

There were many different trades carried on in the town and one way to display them was in a grand procession. On Queen Victoria's birthday on 29 May 1856 the townsfolk took the opportunity to celebrate not only her birthday but also the end of the Crimea War. The parade of trades included Mr Thomas Learwood who made a chair that day and later presented it to the mayor. Learwood invented a 'self acting artificial leg' a couple of years later which became his main business a quarter of a century on as the 'West of England Artificial Limb Manufacturer'. Truro had some unusual trades; there was a kiln on Lemon Quay for lime burning and Mr T.R. Gray had a soap works. In 1880 there was talk of a lead mine in Malabar and the gentlemen interested in starting the venture, about a dozen in all, met at Mr Percy's house where Captain Tonkin cut some blue clay and quartz out of the ground. They felt that this was likely to be lead bearing ground and Mr Pascoe of Chacewater cut the first turf. After pocketing a few samples of the blue clay to show their friends, the men returned to Mr Percy's house for cakes and wine. It seems a very pleasant afternoon was spent by all, probably the most memorable part of the whole venture.

Truro lost another craft about this time. The fact that briar pipes were so cheap meant the the making of clay pipes stopped but when the briars could not be obtained there was no one left with the skill to make the old fashioned clay pipe. They came in a variety of shapes and sizes from a churchwarden to a cutty and it needed quite a skill to make them. In 1883 there were two pipe makers in Truro both called Cock. There were two coopers in town, F. Hawke and J. Neal, and shoe tip manufacturers, Ward and Glasson. On Lemon Quay, J. Beale was a coach maker and advertised, Gigs, Clarences, Sociables etc. all built to order. Lakes Pottery was working in Chapel Hill and continued to do so for many years exporting

Truro Steam Laundry.

Beal's coach factory.

their wares all over the world with the famous square stamp on the bottom of its pots, jugs etc.

Truro suffered less from the outbreak of fires than many towns but during the early part of the century, should a fire break out, the military was available to help out. In 1845 there was a fire in a stable in River Street and it was completely burned down. The newspaper reported that the fire brigade 'was not particularly active' as only one engine could be got out of the coinagehall, which is where they were kept at that time, in less than twenty minutes from the time the alarm bell was sounded. The engine then passed through Boscawen Street and St Nicholas Street 'at a snail's gallop'. By 1876 the Truro Volunteer Fire Brigade had been formed and were so efficient that they narrowly missed winning a national competition in Chester.

Truro was really emerging as a thriving town with all modern conveniences. It now had a police force and a fire brigade, a railway line passing through and its own newspapers to keep the people informed. Then Truro embarked on a new adventure. *The London Gazette* published the following announcement: 'The Queen has been pleased by Letters Patent under the Great Seal of the United Kingdom, bearing the date 28th day of August, 1877, to ordain and declare that the borough of Truro, in the county of Cornwall, shall be a city, and shall be called and styled, 'the City of Truro in the county of Cornwall'.

CHAPTER 7

One hundred years a City

Restoring a bishopric is a slow process and it was in 1847 that Lord John Russell introduced a bill to parliament seeking to introduce three new sees – one of which was to be for Cornwall. It was thrown out and it was another seven years before the Rector of St Columb Major, Dr Walker, offered the advowson and Rector's house at St Columb as a beginning of the endowment of a new bishopric. Shortly after, Bishop Phillpotts of Exeter said that he would gladly give up £500 of his annual income and relinquish his Cornish patronage. After many petitions, committees and letters, Lord Lyttleton succeeded in getting a bill for the formation of three sees including Cornwall through the Lords in 1867 but it failed in the House of Commons. Eventually, after many generous donations, including £40,000 from Lady Rolle, enough money had been found to secure the income required by Parliament and on 15 December 1876 parliament allowed the Bishopric of Truro to be founded. Re-founded would be a better description, however, as we know that Cornwall had its own bishops – starting with Bishop Kenstec in the ninth century. His seat was in Dinnurrin – possibly today's Gerrans in the Truro district.

Once the Bishopric was restored Queen Victoria raised the status of the country market town to a city and a whole new chapter began.

Truro's first bishop was Edward White Benson who later became Archbishop of Canterbury. He oversaw the clearing away of the old St Marys parish church and the subsequent building of the cathedral. For the people of Truro to part with their parish church (the third on the site) was something of a wrench but they wanted the cathedral and agreed to accept the south aisle of the old church as their parish church. They had collected some £3,000-£4,000 to refurbish their church and willingly agreed to it being used for the cathedral instead.

As well as losing all but the south aisle of the parish church, the Georgian Rectory had to come down to make way for the new cathedral. A design by J.P. St Aubyn to enlarge St Marys and turn it into a cathedral was turned down and J.M. Brydon, the architect of several government buildings in London, submitted a plan even though he was not one of the seven architects who were invited to submit. The winning architect was John Loughborough Pearson RA (1817-97). He had already designed several London churches and the Deanery at Lincoln and in Cornwall – the church at Devoran was his design. Pearson decided that as much of

The cathedral before completion, without the two west towers.

Opposite: South aisle of the cathedral part of the old parish church.

the old church was in a poor state of repair, it could go but the south aisle was restored in order to retain it, although the bishop was against 'the tinkering up of rotten stones'. The result is an attractive marriage of the old and new.

On Thursday 20 May 1880 the Prince and Princess of Wales (to us the Duke and Duchess of Cornwall) came to lay the foundation stone. After

Telephone No. 11.

Established Nearly a Century.

The PRINCE'S RESTAURANT

The MOST POPULAR in the City.

Proprietor : - - **C. E. TREGONING.**

Cook, Confectioner, Bread and Biscuit Baker.

Hot Luncheons Daily.

Afternoon Teas a Speciality.

| Separate Tables. | Good Cuisine. | Choice Wines, Ales, &c. |
| Ladies' Tea Room. | Smoking Room. | Lavatories |

CORNISH CLOTTED CREAM,

Packed in Prepared Tasteless Boxes for Parcel Post
in $\frac{1}{2}$lb., $\frac{3}{4}$lb., I$\frac{1}{2}$lbs., and 2lbs.

RUSKS (Unsweetened) for Invalids.

Cornish Macaroons, Heavy Cakes, Pasties.

CONFECTIONERY OF ALL DESCRIPTION.

— Agent for Fuller's —

1 & 2, Duke Street, TRURO.

10

arriving at the railway station at Grampound Road they were taken to Tregothnan, the home of Viscount Falmouth. On the drive into Truro the procession passed under decorative arches designed by architect Silvanus Trevail, past 280 members of the Metropolitan Police and the military. At Southleigh in Lemon Street, the Prince was robed in his masonic attire for the laying of the foundation stone. That the masons were involved did not please everyone but nevertheless the foundation stone for the north-east of the choir was laid with masonic ceremony, as was the second stone – a granite one at the base of a pillar in the nave. It was twenty-three years before that stone was inside the building and it has noticably weathered. It was in October of 1880 that work began to demolish the old parish church. Inevitably this was met with sadness by many as over the years the old church had witnessed many rites of passage – joyful weddings and christenings and solomn funerals of loved ones. The top part of the steeple is preserved today at Diocesan House as is the cross on its top.

The pro-cathedral was a wooden building designed by James Henderson (the grandfather of the historian Charles Henderson). The cost of this building was £430 and it served the people of Truro as a parish church for seven years until the old south aisle was opened again. It seated 400.

The Clerk of the Works for the cathedral was a Londoner called James Bubb who was very enthusiastic about his job. Although some of the locals made it known that they were annoyed at the demolition of the old

Opposite: Advertisement for Prince's restaurant.

Netherton & Worth's
warehouse, Moorfield,
c. 1960.

cottages that got in the way of the new building, he sailed through all the difficulties. He died in 1882 of typhoid and was succeeded by Robert Swain.

Bishop Benson was once accused of draining Cornwall of money as building a cathedral did not come cheap. His reply was 'Yes, but not of zeal' and many Anglicans agreed with him and were pleased that this symbol of the Anglican faith was taking shape. Cornwall had been so swept along by the fervour for John Wesley that the Methodists and other non-conformists outnumbered the people who still clung to the Church of England and Benson's enthusiasm and encouragement helped revive Anglicanism in Cornwall.

In 1883 Bishop Benson was enthroned as Archbishop of Canterbury and Bishop Wilkinson took over in Truro and continued the building programme. Benson came back in 1887 to consecrate the part of the building that was completed and no doubt the new Father Willis organ was tested fully. Benson died in 1896 and, although money was raised and there was a memorial to him in Canterbury, there was no money forthcoming to complete the nave in Truro as a tribute to him, as was hoped. Nevertheless under the direction of J.L. Pearson's son Frank (J.L. had died in 1897) foundations for the nave and two western towers were laid. In 1901 Mr Hawke Dennis offered to pay for the cost of the central tower as a memorial to Queen Victoria who had died that year. By 1910 the two western towers (Edward and Alexandra) were completed – the gift of Mrs Hawkins of Trewithen. The connecting cloister to the

Cathedral School was never built and the planned chapter house did not arrive until the 1960s in modern style and not an octagonal chapter house as originally planned.

Going back to 1877 there were other things going on in the town, not just 'cathedral fever'. By this time the gas works which had been on Lemon Quay since the early part of the century had revolutionised people's lives. Now most of the town had gas lights to illuminate the streets and most of the houses too. A strange thing about the houses was that the gas lighting remained downstairs for some reason – perhaps safety. It was rarely used in the bedrooms where candles or oil lamps were preferred. It was in 1875 that the gas company prepared a catalogue which contained appliances for heating and cooking, before that it was for lighting only.

The shops of the period were not the large national concerns that we have in the town today but small family run businesses often having the living quarters above the shop. 2002 is the centenary of the founding of William A. Vage & Sons, the jewellers, and they are celebrating by giving gold-wrapped chocolate mints to their customers and using commemorative stationery. Most of the shops at the turn of the twentieth century stayed open until 9 p.m. and with the flickering shadows of the naked gas flames (before the days of the gas mantle) they must have been fascinating places with a wealth of commodities among the shadows.

Another business that prospered during the era of the building of the cathedral was the bakery business started by John Cooper Furniss who had his bakery and retail outlet in King Street. He later moved to what

The jewellers' shop (left) *and commemorative stationery* (above) *of William A. Vage & Sons, celebrating their centenary in 2002.*

Roy Wilton and Ron Gallie producing biscuits in the Furniss factory in St Austell Street, c. 1970.

was once Church Lane – now of course Cathedral Lane – and would probably have increased his business even more by feeding the hungry workers. He also kept the passengers on the railway fed and supplied the station buffet. His merchandise would be pushed up Richmond Hill on a handcart when the buffet needed to be re-stocked. John Cooper Furniss formed the company but retired from the board in 1887 and died the following year. He left 100 shares in the company to the City Council to spend the income on coal for citizens of Truro in need but these days the councillors have a hard time trying to find deserving people who still use coal as their fuel.

Truro during the century from 1877 had many varied businesses. The Davey family had a cooperage in Quay Street, W.J. Roberts opened a drapers shop in St Nicholas Street in 1903 which flourished and became a well-known department store in Boscawen Street. Mallet & Sons the ironmongers also had a shop in St Nicholas Street and now trade from Victoria Place and Joseph Pollard set up his bookshop at 5 St Nicholas Street. Mr Pollard catalogued the libraries of several prominent Cornish families and set up a borrowing library above his shop. Occasionally old books can still be found with Pollard's sticker inside the cover but the shop foundered. He died in 1914, closely followed by his son who had expected to take over the business.

Lake's Pottery was flourishing in Chapel Hill and had been through four generations of the same family. Their kiln was on the site of an older one of the seventeenth century and the pottery was still made in the same way. In fact the old kiln was fired using gorse which was brought into Truro from the Redruth and St Agnes areas on drays. Transport was improved enormously with the advent of the railways and even more importantly the standardisation of the gauge used. By 1877, although there was a service which ran from Paddington right down to Penzance, the line was owned by different companies. It was the Cornwall Railway Company that owned the line from Plymouth to Truro and they also owned the line from Truro to Falmouth. The track for these lines was all 7 ft, the broad gauge favoured by Brunel – but the line from Truro to Penzance was owned by the West Cornwall Railway who used the narrow gauge of 4 ft 8½ ins. It was probably a relief to all who had to work on the network when it all became standard gauge in 1892. By 1889 it was all owned by Great Western Railway – often known as God's Wonderful Railway – giving a good service, immaculate railway stations and employment to many.

Truro station was particularly busy and had a thriving marshalling yard. Tourists used to come to the county in droves – and mostly by train. The Cornish Riviera Express and the Cornishman could be relied on to cross the viaduct on time and many people set their watches by the trains. The first viaducts were the Brunel style wooden ones on stone pillars but gradually stone replaced the timber and the new viaduct in Truro was completed in 1905. It was after the Second World War that the shift from rail to private car started and gradually cars overtook the train for popularity. In the 1960s Truro still had quite a number of people employed at the station but, as the goods section was gradually run down and the passenger numbers dropped, so the staff numbers fell. Much of the magic of the trains was lost when the service was nationalised and steam had to

Truro locomotive depot, c. 1950.

give way to diesel. Before the wars 'special trains' were often put on for outings or an exhibition and Sunday School trips were regularly transported by specially hired trains.

Over the years peoples' ideas of entertainment changed. In the late 1870s people had regular visits from the fair at Whitsun and the circus also came annually. A magic lantern show always proved a strong attraction at the public rooms where there was also a regular supply of concerts and plays. Over the years various clubs and societies were formed. The cricket club had been formed in 1810 and was still going strong in 1900 when their games were played at Tremorvah. Ship owner Mr Chellew was a patron of the club but when differences occurred with the club after the war, he stopped them playing there and it is said he made his point by building a wall across the pitch! The Truro City Football Club was formed in 1889 and the Rugby Club, which folded during the First World War, was re-formed in the 1920s. Women were not left out; the Womens' Institute in Truro was one of the first in the county when it formed in 1918. People were able to enjoy their leisure more because standards of living had improved, although by today's standards they were still not good. The agriculture industry had been hit hard by cheaper grain from America which meant there was little point in growing it here. The bottom had dropped out of the copper market and tin mining was mostly deep mining and not very lucrative, only giving employment to a small number of those looking for work. The fishing industry was thriving but the old toast of 'Copper, Tin and Fish' was hardly appropriate any more. Many of the ordinary people were underfed and terrified of the diseases which could suddenly take hold and cause untold numbers of deaths. Dr Clement Carlyon's policy of keeping the town clean was improved upon, cess pits were removed, almost two miles of pipes were added to the sewers and the pigs that people liked to keep as pets (or winter food supplies) were moved away from the residential areas. It was ironic that there was typhoid in the infirmary in 1878 which claimed the wife of the house surgeon. The infirmary had a sewer going past the building but was not connected to it!

In 1875 the Truro Water Company was founded – another step in the right direction for better public health and by the end of the nineteenth century the town had proper sewers and the houses were connected to them. However, it was not until the 1930s that the treatment works at Newham was built to stop the discharge of raw sewage into the rivers. Together with the twice-weekly collection of refuse beginning in 1919 things really began to improve.

As well as the infirmary, Truro had a charity called the 'Public Dispensary' which was run by a committee and provided medical care and medicines for the needy. Those who were in need could obtain a letter

Tregolls Manor, formerly St Paul's Church of England Infants school.

from a committee member and it entitled them to six weeks treatment. It sounded good and so it was for those who were lucky enough to benefit but even with the infirmary the medical care was inadequate to meet the needs of all those who deserved it.

More houses were being built; Waterloo Terrace was built by the council after the First World War. The houses were for rent, the most common way of occupying a house at this time, not many people could afford to buy, and at 4/6d per week the people who really needed the houses couldn't even afford to rent them. W.J. Burley tells us in his centenary book that in the century 1877-1977 the number of houses had risen from approximately 1,600 to 5,000 and at the same time the population had grown from 11,000 to 16,000.

As the population was growing and gradually improving in health and wealth so the need for more and better education was growing. The old grammar school with the wonderful reputation for teaching the classics and educating some of Cornwall's most famous sons was in its closing days. By 1877 the old school was no longer fit for use, although in 1863, £40 had been spent on it: drainage was installed, a new store added and general decoration undertaken. After moving to various premises and being re-formed it became the Cathedral School.

Truro had its share of Church of England schools, St Mary's, St John's, St Georges and St Pauls Infants and also British Schools which were the non-conformist equivalent. A Mr Edward Truncheon ran a 'Ragged School' in Campfield Hill for the very deprived and also there were so-called 'dame schools' around the town. The house now occupied by Mrs Clarice Mortensen Fowler in Rosewin Row was one such school and had the schoolroom on the first floor. It is known that many young men were trained there in the copperplate writing necessary to be clerks in the various solicitor's offices in the town. Truro also had a training college known as the Church of England Training College for Girls. It was founded in 1858 and continued for many years in a building which dominated the skyline in Agar Road.

The Education Act of 1870, which stated that there must be a place at school for every child, and the knowledge that education would soon be compulsory, pulled all the educational outlets together. St Marys school moved to new premises, St Pauls opened in 1896, the infants at the bottom of Agar Road and the juniors at the top and the old British Schools were replaced by Bosvigo. The Wesleyan School of St Marys continued near the chapel.

Secondary education also changed. The Wesleyans opened their new boarding school for boys in 1880 under the name Truro College but which is now known as Truro School. The new diocese was strengthening and opened establishments for girls: Truro High School for Girls in 1897 and the County Grammar School for Girls in 1906 with Daniell Road set up in 1911 to replace the Weslyan school. The Central Technical School in Union Place was the gift of John Passmore Edwards, as was the library which benefitted all.

Passmore Edwards was a local success story. He was born in the village of Blackwater, near Truro, in 1823 of a Cornish father and a Devonshire lady called Susan Passmore from Newton Abbot. His father was a carpenter and he had a humble upbringing but went off to London to seek

Former Dame School in Rosewin Row.

Truro School.

Truro County School for Girls, now demolished to make way for a supermarket.

his fortune. He had first tried Manchester as the agent for a London newspaper *The Sentinel* but things did not work out, so in 1850 he bought the monthly magazine called *The Public Good* but it failed and he was declared bankrupt. This would have finished many other people. He lived a very frugal life for the next ten years and worked long and hard. Gradually his lot improved and when he became the owner of *The Mechanics Magazine* and *The Building News* both magazines began to do well. This was the basis of his fortune as the magazines were particularly useful to the working class and priced within their means. The first thing he did was pay his old creditors who were so delighted that they treated him to a celebration dinner. Before long John Passmore Edwards was endowing schools, hospitals, working men's institutes and libraries not

Passmore Edwards' Free Library and Technical School for Boys.

only in Cornwall, but in London, Kent, Surrey, in fact anywhere he could help. The library and school in Truro were built in 1899 and the architect was another Cornishman, Silvanus Trevail. He was born in the village of Luxulyan and was well known for designing public buildings such as schools, churches and chapels. He worked in Lemon Street in Truro from the early 1880s for twenty years and it was while he was the mayor that he obtained the funds for the new library from Passmore Edwards.

Religion also played a part in educating. In the Centenary book Mr Burley tells us that his grandmother decided to educate herself after bringing up her family and she went to chapel 'for the needs of the spirit and to church to learn how to say words right'. Truro now had a cathedral under construction, St Johns, St Georges and St Pauls churches as well as Kenwyn up on the hill and St Clement down by the river. The Methodists had purchased the land where the Vivians' town house had once been and Philip Sambell designed the chapel which stands there

today. St Georges Methodist arose from another group of Wesleyans who at one time used the building in Kenwyn Street which later became the Salvation Army Citadel. Over the years a United Methodist Church was formed from the other groups which included the New Connection Methodists and the Bible Christians. Truro even had a chapel at the top of Campfield Hill called 'The Shouters'. When the Reverend John Boyle left the Methodist Connection and formed the Bible Christians he set up societies in many different places and at Porth Kea he built a schoolroom which doubled as a chapel. This society later joined the Brianites and had a chapel in Truro. Two ladies – sisters called Miss Downes – joined the sect but, although very religious, they would shout and scream during the services. This upset the rest of the congregation and the ministers asked them to desist but they refused, so they formed the Shouters and built their own chapel at their own expense. They were joined by many others but on the death of the elder Miss Downes the Shouters ceased to be.

The Baptists also had a church, another Sambell building in River Street and the Primitive Methodists used to meet in Walsingham Place before they built their own church in Kenwyn Street. The Salvation Army's citadel in Kenwyn Street had been used by other sects for worship before them. At one time Billy Bray was a regular preacher there.

In 1884 Reverend Father John Grainger personally bought a plot of land at the end of Dereham Terrace where he built a Roman Catholic Church to replace their previous building. It served them well until Our Lady of the Portal and St Piran – an echo of that chapel of a former age – was built in St Austell Street in 1972.

Bill head of local blacksmiths and farriers from the 1970s. For fifty years before that they had worked at 108 Kenwyn Street where the yard of the smithy was laid with cobblestones by the friars.

The old Roman Catholic Church in Chapel Hill.

The Britannia Inn.

Although Truro was one of the very first places in the country to have a gas works – electricity took much longer to reach the town, though it was not for the want of trying. The idea was first talked about in 1890 and the council first asked for a scheme to be prepared ten years later. The initial proposal by Headley of St Austell involved not only lighting but also a tramway. The tramway was turned down and the lighting part of it referred to the Cab and Lighting Committee but it sank from sight. It was not until 19 October 1927 that Mrs Lodge, wife of the chairman of the Electric Lighting Committee switched on the supply.

It was decided during the 1920s that the river should be covered over between Lemon Quay and Back Quay and when it was done, in two stages, it dramatically altered the face of the town. No longer could fairly large ships come right up into the heart of town, although they could still come up as far as The Green, where Green House which housed the customs office sat looking down the river and its occupant was available to collect all dues. The Green was in fact a bowling green and there was also an alley for skittles behind the Britannia Inn. Quite near, on the junction of Quay Street and Princes Street, stood ,and, in fact, still stands Truro's Penfold pillar box. It is of a design that was only in use for thirteen

A ship in Truro River c. 1960.

years and is much loved by the locals – although as it faces a building it is almost impossible to photograph.

On 15 October 1922 the war memorial was unveiled in Boscawen Street. Truro had lost its fair share of soldiers during the First World War and more names were added to it after the Second World War. In 1914 most people thought that 'it would be over by Christmas' but as time went on, and more and more wounded were shipped home, a gloomy air descended on the town where many of the injured were cared for. The infirmary was fully stretched and emergency centres were established in Sunday schools and the workhouse. When people are down it seems more things go wrong and in November 1914 the town hall suffered a fire which caused the tower of the town clock to come crashing down into the council chamber beneath. Fortunately no-one was hurt and an anonymous donor paid for a new clock tower identical to the original except that the new clock face was white, not black.

During the Second World War, on 6 August 1942 two bombs were dropped on Truro. One hit the infirmary and one exploded over Agar Road, not much when compared to some of the larger cities, but twelve people were killed that day. Some children had just come home from a Sunday school outing. Dennis Mitchell, who had been sent into the backyard of 23 Kenwyn Street to empty sand out of his socks and shoes, found himself suddenly pinned to the ground by his father as the enemy plane which had just strafed the playing field at Hendra flew over and left bullet holes in the yard wall. Many Truro people made their contribution to the war effort at H.T.P. Motors Ltd on Lemon Quay where aircraft parts were repaired, especially those from Spitfires.

After the war the town continued to adapt and change and gradually the market town which had become a city became popular with people from 'up country' who were able to buy property much cheaper than they could in the big towns and cities. The town became crowded with cars and the river which had been covered in the 1920s at Lemon Quay and Back Quay became a well-used car park. Some things did not change and the Truronians were justly proud of their wide and elegant Boscawen Street with the beautiful old Red Lion Inn facing up Lemon Street. Then came that fateful day in July 1967 when a lorry careered down Lemon Street out of control and ran into the front of it. The Red Lion had to be demolished and something special was gone forever.

Back Quay and the Green, c. 1960.

The Mayor of Truro, J. Arnold Hodge, shows Lynne Warmington the workings of the town clock in 1967.

CHAPTER 8
Into the Twenty-First Century

Although Launceston was the gateway to Cornwall and the most important town in the time of the Black Prince and even though Bodmin became the county town where the assize court was held, these days Truro has become the administrative centre for Cornwall. The County Hall is in Truro, the new law courts, opened in 1988 are on Castle Hill and the cathedral is the focus of the Anglican faith in the county.

In 1977, the centenary of the city, the queen visited as part of her Silver Jubilee celebrations and again as part of her Golden Jubilee tour of the country. It was interesting to find that at the funeral of Queen Elizabeth, the Queen Mother, the hymn 'Immortal, Invisible God Only Wise' was sung as it was one of her favourites. It was written by Walter Chalmers Smith (1824-1908) who was the architect of St Georges Methodist church and a member of the family who had the shop Criddle & Smith in Truro. Many fine pieces of furniture were purchased from them or restored by them.

Changes to the town since 1977 have been many and varied but thankfully the heart of the town is largely unchanged. The City Hall, which for many years housed the Regent Cinema, then later became a theatre and a venue for prize-givings, etc, has, after many years of plans and set-backs, been transformed into the Hall for Cornwall. Not only is it

The Law Courts, opened in 1988 on the site of the cattle market, and before that the Truro castle.

used as a theatre but the moveable tiers of seats mean that flea markets, bazaars and Women's Institute sales can still be held for the enjoyment of all. A new fly tower has been built on the municipal building but otherwise, from the outside, the structure is basically unchanged. Outside there is a new piazza – still requiring modification to keep pedestrians and public transport safe from each other – built on the site which was a tidal river at the beginning of the twentieth century and a car park for many years in recent memory. Many people would have liked to have the river opened up again to be able to sit on its banks under an avenue of trees. Unfortunately once the main road, Morlaix Avenue, was built in the 1960s it stopped the river at Back Quay and Lemon Quay being flushed out by the tide. The Cornish mud, which contains mining deposits, would have become somewhat aromatic! Morlaix Avenue replaced Boscawen Bridge, the first one being a wooden structure built in 1849 and later replaced by a second, stone one in 1862.

Some wonderful buildings have been lost to the city over the last quarter of a century, Truro County School for Girls was one. High over the town on Treyew Road and opposite the new county hall, it saw several generations of girls pass through its doors but was demolished to make way for a supermarket in 1993. Other buildings that have gone include the

The mayor alights from his boat to beat the water bounds, 1967.

Coach & Horses in Pydar Street, Roberts' department store in Boscawen Street, the bus station on Lemon Quay and City Hospital has closed with the fate of the building unknown. Of course changes like these are inevitable but if too many occur gradually each town will lose its individuality.

The local government reorganisation in 1974 formed the new Carrick District Council and took away most of the powers of the City Council but Truro still has its mayor and councillors and much of the ceremony attached to that office brings history to life. The charter from Elizabeth I in 1589 gave Truro control over the river, including the harbour at Falmouth, but in 1661, when Falmouth received its own charter, it took control of its own harbour. Truro disputed this but the matter was decided by the courts in 1709 and the river was divided. Truro's jurisdiction ended at Messack Point and Tarra Point.

The importance of the river to Truro is self-evident. Indeed, beating the river bounds is a ceremony still carried out every six years by the Mayor of Truro. The letters TB (Truro boundary) are re-cut by the mayor in the boundary marker which is a large granite obelisk. By doing this he is re-asserting Truro's authority over the river to this point. A small ceremony is performed when the 'arrest' of a citizen for a debt of £999 19s 11½d is also acted out. In 1969, when Councillor J. Arnold Hodge was mayor, the two people 'arrested and bailed' were Donald Vage and Murray Smith, just to prove that Truro has jurisdiction over the area. Another reference to Truro's authority over the river is the pair of silver oars presented to the mayor at the mayor-making. As Truro owes its existence to its growth around the three rivers it is appropriate that these ceremonies continue to the present day.

The modern version of Boscawen Bridge which carries Morlaix Avenue over the River Allen.

WALKING TOUR

Walking Tour

We start and end our walk at High Cross and follow a roughly circular walk round the centre of the town. It is all level walking except for a few steps which lead down to one of our local opeways although this is easily by-passed. For anyone walking at a normal pace the walk will take about one hour.

> **Start your walk by standing beside the old wayside cross at High Cross.**

This is believed to be the oldest part of Truro and where the cross has stood for many hundreds of years. Looking at the cross itself it is easy to see the join between the shaft and the wheel headed cross. Back in the 1950s workmen were digging up St Nicholas Street when they found a

Plan of the city centre.

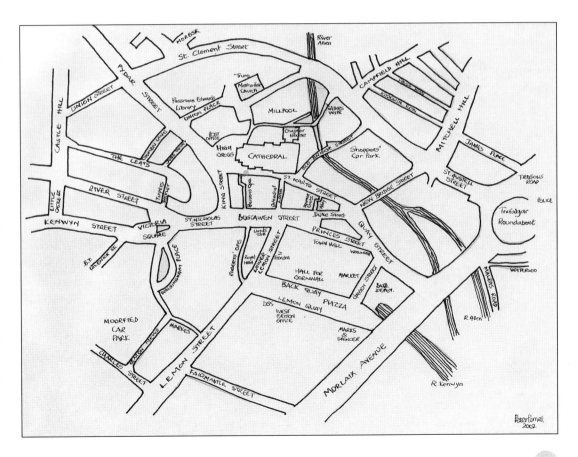

Walking Tour

St Mary's Street.

piece of granite remarkably similar to the shaft of this cross. Thinking it was just rubble or infill they carried on their work. A few days later they found another piece of granite; the top of the cross. The Curator of the museum was sent for and identified it as the original cross from High Cross. It was placed near the west doors of the cathedral in High Cross and stayed there for about fifty years until Councillor John Christie, the mayor at the time, commissioned a new shaft and had it restored to its proper position.

> **Facing the cathedral turn to the left to look at the building which is now Blewetts the Bakers.**

This beautiful building was once the assembly rooms where all manner of balls and entertainments took place. Many of the prominent local families had country estates and town houses and the winter programme at the assembly rooms meant that these families stayed in their town houses during the winter so that they could enjoy each others company and all the concerts and dances that were on offer. The plaques are Wedgewood and Thalia, the muse of comedy, watches over the building. The other two plaques represent Shakespeare and Garrick. Although only the facade now remains it gives an idea of High Cross in the late 1700s. As related earlier, the money for the building was raised by tontine at £55

per share. Lord Falmouth was allowed to buy three shares but the remaining twenty-five shares were allocated one per person with each purchaser nominating a life. Due to a slip up, the lives were not nominated for a few years and when they were, a man called John James nominated his five-year-old granddaughter, Eliza. She was still living 100 years after the assembly rooms opened its doors to the public, so in 1889, as the last nominated life left alive, she inherited it all.

> *Now walk to the left of the cathedral and follow the path until you reach the building now used for the Social Services.*

This building has been left with the brickwork unfinished as it was intended to join it to the cathedral when finances permitted. It was built as part of the Cathedral School (founded in 1906) which grew out of the old grammar school believed to have been founded in 1549. The building in front of you was in use as part of the school from 1909-1960 and has a plaque on the wall. After this the school moved to Trewinnard Court at Kenwyn but closed in 1982. On your right is the chapter house built in

Wedgewood plaques on the Assembly Rooms, depicting Thalia, Shakespeare and Garrick.

Walking Tour

Former Cathedral School, now the Social Services Department.

the 1960s. It was intended to complete the cathedral with a 'Noble octagonal Chapter House and a cloister to the north of the church' but it never materialised. The current chapter house is well used as a refectory and is also available to hire for evening meetings, etc.

Continue along the walkway until you reach a pool on your left.

This is the Millpool, part of the Manor Mill and used for grinding corn. Behind the pool is a road (St Austell Street) and situated just on the other side of the road is the area of Truro Vean where around 1800 Truro had a carpet factory. The noise of the spinning jennies was reported to be

very loud but as the factory provided employment for many people, even those who were disabled and would not otherwise have been able to fend for themselves, no one minded too much.

> *Following the river, with the cathedral on your right, continue down Wilkes Walk. The River Allen is flowing along beside you and on your left is the Barley Sheaf public house.*

The Barley Sheaf is on the site of the dyeing works for the carpet factory. No doubt the river was a necessary part of the dyeing process but it probably caused some pollution. Wilkes Walk is named after a Town

The River Allen leaving the Millpool and flowing towards the old Sunday School of St Mary's.

101

Walking Tour

Part of the old Truro Grammar School.

Clerk of Truro who was tragically killed in a road accident. It leads into Old Bridge Street.

> *Cross over the road and turn left then first right into an alleyway leading to the 'Bay of Bengal' Indian restaurant. This brings you into the shoppers car park. Turn to the right and stop on the footbridge over the river facing the back of the Royal British Legion Club.*

On your right is the old bridge. It has the square design of a typical medieval bridge and was formerly known as the East Bridge. This carried the road out of Truro in the St Austell direction and it was in this area that the old chapel with the unusual dedication 'blessed Mary of Portell' was situated. Beyond the bridge is the old St Mary's Sunday School Building. Behind you is the bridge known as 'New Bridge' which was built in 1775.

> *Cross the footbridge and go to the right of the club where there is an alleyway which brings you out into St Marys Street. Look to the right at the cathedral.*

Opposite: Looking up St Mary's Street in 1912.

Walking Tour

New Bridge Street.

Most noticeable is the green turret of the clock tower coated in Cornish copper. The clock was taken away many years ago as it became dangerous. The aisle which borders the street is St Marys aisle, the one remaining part of the old parish church which was renovated and incorporated into the new building when the rest of the old church was pulled down. The first church on the site was dedicated in 1259 by Bishop Bronescombe who came down from Exeter for the occasion. He went over to the Kenwyn Street area of town and dedicated a chapel for the Dominican friars there and also went up to Kenwyn to re-dedicate the church there. As the cathedral was built right in the heart of town there were fears that the noise of traffic would disturb the services, so the road was made of wooden setts to muffle the sound of hooves and wheels. They can still be seen near the kerb whenever the modern tarmac starts to erode but, as they were extremely slippery when wet, there was no public outcry when they were covered.

Turn away from the cathedral and walk a few steps .

Look at the building with the bell tower on top. This is part of the old grammar school founded by Walter Borlase in 1549, a building where many famous Cornishmen were educated. This particular building was in use from 1700-1877. Through these doors passed, among others: Humphry Davy, inventor of the miner's safety lamp; Henry Martyn,

missionary and translator of the bible into several languages; Richard and John Lander who discovered the source of the River Niger and Goldsworthy Gurney whose steam carriages required the standardisation of time across the country so timetables had meaning.

Next, walk to the end of the street and into the square.

If you are lucky you will see 'Uncle Albert' resting in his chair while his wife does some shopping in Vage's jewellers shop. 2002 is the centenary year of this family firm and it is thriving still. Inside is a photograph of the shop window after a smash and grab raid in 1911. Mr Vage gave chase as he was in the store at the time but he stopped to put on his hat and coat before he went out as he could not let his standards slip! Despite the delay, two tramps were arrested. Later, during the First World War Mr Vage's nephew fell into conversation in the trenches and amazingly he discovered that he was talking to one of the tramps responsible.

On the left is the New Bridge with a public house at the end of it now called 'The Crab & Ale House'. Although the brewery changed its name in the last few years, it did have the distinction of being the longest

The Truro pub which retained its name for the longest period, The White Hart Inn, recently renamed the Crab & Ale House.

surviving pub to keep its original name as it was the custom for publicans to take the name of their pub with them when they moved premises. It still has the words 'White Hart' painted on the badge on the wall but the hart itself has been painted out.

> *Continue straight across the road into the narrow street called Quay Street and walk to the end. Turn right towards the telephone kiosk and post box.*

The Victorian post box is one of the type known as a Penfold Box, one of only a few still in existence. They were only made for thirteen years between 1866-1879. While facing the box, look forward to the building on your right which is part of the Royal Bank of Scotland. This was once the town house of the Rosewarne family and it was here that Pitt the Younger was entertained. Later, when the house was in the hands of Sewell Stokes, the first clerk to the county council, Alfred Lord Tennyson visited.

Opposite: *The Victorian 'Penfold' pillar box.*

Below: *The Palace Buildings with Green Street.*

Walking Tour

Cross the road to the house just mentioned and, keeping it on your right, walk to the corner and cross the road ahead of you, Green Street.

The building now in front of you is known as Bishop Philpott's library, although it is now a clothes shop and the library of rare books used by the clergy is now housed at Diocesan House at Kenwyn. The stained-glass window which once graced the building is also up at Kenwyn with an electric light placed behind it to show the effect of the light pouring through the glass. In order to make Green Street wider some of the buildings were demolished and there is a plaque on the wall commemorating the Fighting Cocks Inn where Richard and John Lander were born. The family crest was a dolphin and there was a curled dolphin carved in stone set in the wall of the house. When the building was knocked down, the dolphin was removed to Boscawen Park in Malpas Road and can be seen there.

Walk to the front of the building, known as the Palace Buildings after a cinema that was once situated there, and look across the road.

Opposite the front of the Palace Buildings is a house known as the Old Mansion House. This was built around 1700 for the Enys family who made their money out of smelting. When it was built it backed on to its own quay in one of the busiest parts of town. Just along the road from the Palace Buildings is the Britannia Inn. Not only did it once have an indoor bowling alley but it backed on to the bowling green, hence the name 'The

Plaque in Green Street on the wall of the old Bishop Philpott's library.

ADJOINING THIS BUILDING STOOD THE FIGHTING COCKS INN WHERE RICHARD LANDER THE CORNISH EXPLORER WAS BORN ON 8TH FEBRUARY 1804.

The Britannia Inn.

Green' for the area behind it. For many years the Britannia was owned by the borough but was sold in order to finance a new swimming pool which was built at Hendra but after a lifespan of over twenty years the pool was closed in favour of the new one at Gloweth.

> **Retrace your steps past the Palace Buildings, cross Green Street walk past the old town house of the Rosewarnes and with the Penfold box behind you look at Princes House.**

Princes House was built in 1740 for William Lemon whose country estate was at Carclew (between Truro and Falmouth). William Lemon was the son of a poor man but rose to great wealth through his hard work, shrewd investments and successful marriage.

The house was designed by Thomas Edwards and saw some grand entertaining but, because he also wanted a country house, Mr Lemon employed Mr Edwards to design that as well. Continuing along Princes Street, the next house of interest is the Mansion House built in 1760 for Thomas Daniell, manager and successor to William Lemon. The front of the house is faced with Bath stone from the quarries of Ralph Allen, known as 'The Man of Bath'. He was Mrs Daniell's uncle and the stone

Walking Tour

Duke Street and the bank now known as Coinagehall.

was a generous wedding present. Ralph Allen was a Cornishman born in St Blazey who made his fortune by modernising the postal service and was well able to afford such a fine present from his quarries at Coombe Down. The Daniells called their son Ralph Allen Daniel as a tribute to him.

> **Keep walking in the same direction until you come to Woolworths and stand with your back towards the shop facing Boscawen Street.**

In front of you and slightly to your right is a building in the Tudor style called 'The Coinagehall'. It was actually built as a bank but is slightly unusual as the vaults are upstairs. It is so named because it stands on the site of the old coinage hall built in 1351. Truro was a stannary town and the tin was brought here to be assayed in the coinagehall. If it passed the test for purity it would be stamped with the arms of the duchy and the relevant tax paid. The smelters would have already stamped the ingots with their own mark. Often the lamb and flag was used as a symbol of purity especially if the tin was to be exported to a Roman Catholic country. The pelican and the phoenix also figured as smelter's marks. Above the old coinagehall were rooms leased by the council and let for various purposes such as banquets and entertainments. The old building was pulled down in 1848. Boscawen Street is as wide as it is because, when Middle Row (which dated from the same time as the coinagehall) was demolished, it was decided not to build anything else there. Market Street and Fore Street therefore became one and the new street was named for a member of Lord Falmouth's family, Admiral Edward Boscawen whose nickname was 'Old Dreadnought'. Where Woolworths now stands was once the principal inn of the town, The Bull. In the 1630s the innkeeper was Edward Castle who owned plenty of silver and silver gilt, had a well stocked wine cellar and the rooms of the inn had their own names such as Dolphin, Rose, Helmet and Phoenix. Being so

An elegant doorway in Boscawen Street.

Boscawen Street, 1912.

close to the coinagehall, this inn would have been well used, especially during the twice yearly coinages.

> **Walking further along the street with the war memorial (erected in 1922) on your right you come to the Italianate style municipal buildings.**

The architect was Christopher Eales and the building was constructed in 1846. Above is the town hall and Council Chamber with an information bureau on the ground floor. The Hall for Cornwall uses the rear of the building but when a show or market is taking place it is possible to enter from the front.

> **Walk under one of the arches and head towards the wall on the far right.**

It may be gloomy here but you should be able to make out a stone tablet on the wall which used to be in the old market house in Middle Row. It was placed in storage when that building was demolished until it could be re-erected here. Written (or rather, carved) by order of Jenkin Daniell, Mayor, it exhorts people to use fair measure and not cheat.

Carved are the words 'Who seks to find eternal tresure must use no guile in waight or measure 1615'.

> **_Returning to Boscawen Street, turn left as you come out of the archway._**

Looking at the Co-Op on the opposite side of the road, try to visualise the beautiful old Red Lion which stood there until a runaway lorry demolished it in the 1960s. It was built as a town house for the Foote family and was later taken over as an inn when the Red Lion of the day became too dilapidated for use. Mr Edward Giddy put an advertisement in the Sherborne Mercury announcing that he was leaving the business and closing up the Red Lion, then Thomas Gatty declared that he would be the new landlord and that he was opening up the business at the house called Mr Foot's Great House.

> **_Walk to the corner of Boscawen Street and Lower Lemon Street and turn left. With Lloyds Bank on the right and the sports shop on the left walk to the end of the street, turn left and pause at the top of the piazza._**

Where you are standing is the former site of the bridge built to replace stepping stones when Lemon Street was constructed. The bridge succumbed to development when the river was covered over and a car

The new piazza joining Back Quay and Lemon Quay.

Walking Tour

park built in 1926. The car park survived until 2001 when work began on the new piazza. Looking up Lemon Street, the finest Georgian Street west of Bath, you can see Lander's monument at the top. Nevill Northey Burnard carved the statue after the death of Richard Lander (who discovered the source of the River Niger) using Lander's young daughter as the model. The column is one of the many features of Truro designed by the deaf-mute architect Philip Sambell. By the time the monument was complete, Richard's brother John, who accompanied him to Africa, was dead as well so he is included on the inscription. The houses in Lemon Street were built 1800-1830, with St John's church (the dome is

Lemon Street.

King Street.

Walking Tour

visible on the left) another Sambell design, built in 1828. Now looking down the piazza and up to the skyline you can see the clock tower and buildings of Truro School, a Methodist school which started life as Truro College. The headmaster of the school is a member of the Headmaster's Conference. Turning round now to look at the building behind you, what is now the Royal Hotel was once a staging post hotel built in 1800 and called Pearce's Hotel.

The Quicksilver coach used to leave Falmouth each day bound for London and arrive at Pearce's for a late lunch. From here it was on to Launceston for dinner and London several days later. It was after a visit from Prince Albert in 1846 that the name of the hotel was changed to The Royal. Although Queen Victoria was with Prince Albert on the tour, she stayed on board the Royal Yacht at Malpas.

> **To the left of the Royal Hotel is an alleyway between the hotel and the public toilets. This is known as Roberts Ope (pronounced op). You go down over the steps and follow the path alongside the river Kenwyn and come out at the other end in Boscawen Street once more.**

Opposite you will see Littlewoods which occupies most of the former site of the Robartes family great house. It extended back a long way, almost up to the church which was where the cathedral is now. Some of this building, constructed in the 1580s, survived until 1960 when it had to make way for the Midland Bank (now HSBC) and to allow Littlewoods to be extended.

Part of The Leats leading to Victoria Gardens.

Continue along Boscawen Street past the opening of King Street on your right and walk down St Nicholas Street.

This street is named after the Fraternity of St Nicholas, a group of traders who formed themselves into a guild known to have existed in 1278. Somewhere under the street is the shaft of the wayside cross which is now in High Cross and believed to be the original. When workmen were digging up the road in the 1950s, they found a large piece of granite which they covered over and left there. It was only later when the wheel-headed cross appeared in their excavations that they sent for Mr Douch, the curator of the museum who identified it.

At the end of St Nicholas Street you come to Victoria Square, although the correct name is Victoria Place.

This is the site of the old West Bridge. According to reports it was a narrow v-shaped structure with the river Kenwyn flowing underneath.

Standing with your back to Malletts Hardware store, look across the road to the right to a shop called D2. This is the site of the town mill powered by the leat called Tregeare Water. This mill was essential to the castle and pounded away relentlessly. In front of you and towards the left is an area of land forming a rough triangle where the friars settled when they came to Truro in the middle of the thirteenth century. An approximation of the area used by them would be between Kenwyn Street (on the left), River Street (in front and to the right) and the road that joins them, Little Castle Street. The friary was believed to be in existence from 1259-1536.

Turn and face Malletts and look to the left of the shop.

There are two lanes here. The one for you to see is on the left and is called Walsingham Place. No one is quite sure who the architect was but it is quite possible that it was again Philip Sambell who left his mark on Truro with his beautiful buildings. Although built as houses, currently all except one are used as office space. Walsingham Place was a favourite with John Betjeman.

If desired you can turn left at the top of Walsingham Place and cross the service road at the back of the Somerfield car park to Lemon Street Market. As this little building which used to be stabling is due for renovation it may not be there after publication but hopefully it will survive. Inside, on the floor, is the turntable which was used to turn carriages so that they could exit into Lemon Street, the same way they came in.

Great Western Railway seat in Victoria Gardens, donated by Mr.Kingdon in memory of his wife.

Walking Tour

The park-keeper's house and exit to the law courts, Victoria Gardens.

> **Retrace your steps to Victoria Square and walk up River Street and stop opposite the museum.**

The museum is another Sambell building. It was built as a savings bank in 1845 but later became a school of mines. It was sold to the Royal Institution for £1,800. The right end of the museum was originally the Baptist chapel and also a Philip Sambell building. The ground floor of that part of the building is now a cafeteria. It was bought by the Royal Institution some years ago and has had an extension built to join the two buildings together.

> **Cross over to the same side of the road as the museum and continue up River Street for a few more yards until you can turn right.**

You are now in Castle Street. Look up to the top of the hill and you will see the new law courts, opened in 1988. This was the site of Truro's castle and the top part of the street is called Castle Hill. The castle was granted to Richard de Lucy in 1140 and it is to him that the rise of Truro is attributed. It was already a vacant plot in 1270 and by Leland's time (1506-1552) was a 'playing and shoting place'. In 1840 a cattle market was built here but it has now been moved to the outskirts of the town on the Newquay Road. When the cattle market was under construction, the walls of the castle were found, but they were just earthworks, any stone that had been there was gone. The castle may have been an adulterine castle thrown up in the civil strife between Stephen and Matilda or possibly an older earthwork may have pre-dated it on the site.

Walking Tour

At this point it is possible to extend the walk if anyone would like to see the park and possibly sit down for a rest Opposite Elizabeth House, the job centre, is a narrow traffic free lane. Cross the road at the end (Edward Street) and continue along the traffic-free walk known as The Leats to the waterfall gardens on the left, under the railway viaduct, and to the entrances to Victoria gardens which are on the right and reached by slabs of granite across the Kenwyn. The gardens were opened in 1898, the year of Queen Victoria's Diamond Jubilee. By walking up through the gardens and looking for the cottage which once housed the park keeper and his wife it is possible to exit beside the law courts. The view from their walls looks right out over the town and down the river. It is then easy to come down the hill to the place where you are now standing.

Turn right and walk along this part of the Leats, which is unfortunately no longer traffic free. As this is the service road for shops such as W.H. Smith and several electrical shops care must be taken as lorries and other traffic use it.

Arched doorway of the old Congregational church, The Leats.

Walking Tour

Just past the entrance to Pydar Mews, on the opposite side, there is an arched doorway. This is the only remaining sign that the building beside the doorway facing out on to River Street was once the Congregational chapel. In old photographs it even had turrets on the roof but these days you would never guess at its past.

> **Behind you is the back of W.H. Smith with a lane beside it. Walk down this lane.**

The water from the leats runs along beside you and the shops on your right have the traditional slabs to cross the water. This is called Coombes

Coombes Lane.

Walking Tour

A building in Pydar Street parts of which dates back to 1650.

Lane. There used to be a shirt making factory here and also a school called 'Old Pascoe's' which the young Richard Lander attended.

At the end of this lane you emerge into Pydar Street.

Pydar Street is thought to be the oldest street in Truro and was where those who were crossing the county from the River Gannel to the River Fal came down into the town. It is named after the hundred (administrative area) of Pydar to which it leads. Looking towards the town on your right is 7 Pydar Street which is a very old building. Today it is the Orange mobile phone shop but if you can visualise the frontage without any of the modern signs, it is just as it was in 1750. Parts of the

Walking Tour

Passmore Edwards' Free Library.

building date from as long ago as 1650, although it has been altered over the years. It was a solicitor's office from 1853 to 1987.

> **Now with your back to no. 7 look at the public library.**

You can see the end of the building as it fronts on to Union Place. The money for the building of a library and technical school, which is what the far end of the building was formerly used for, was donated by John Passmore Edwards. He was a great public benefactor who not only endowed libraries, hospitals, schools and institutes in his native Cornwall, but also in London, Kent, Surrey and Devon. He made his money in the publishing world and wanted to bring knowledge within the reach of

Truro Methodist church.

High Cross.

Walking Tour

Foundation stone of Passmore library and Technical School.

everyone. The architect of the building was Silvanus Trevail, another Cornishman, who designed many buildings in Truro in the late nineteenth century, the most famous of which was the post office in High Cross (now demolished).

Now look down Union Place to the end.

The Methodist chapel, once known as St Mary Clement but today simply known as Truro Methodist, is another of Philip Sambell's designs. It was erected in 1830 on the site part owned by both the borough and the Robartes family. It was leased to the Vivian family in the eighteenth century and it was here that John and Betsy Vivian lived in their town house and welcomed home their son, General Hussey Vivian, after the battle of Waterloo. His mother Betsy (née Cranch) had been a very pretty girl and had many suitors before her marriage. When she finally accepted John Vivian, the boys of the old grammar school were alarmed to hear a gun shot and discover that one of their masters had killed himself. Dr Hopson was one of her disappointed suitors. Mrs Vivian would have been very distressed by this herself, as she was loved by most people for her sweet nature and joy in life. Behind the house were orchards and the particular type of apples that flourished here were called Cornish Gillyflowers. They were so popular with King George III that every year boxes of them were sent up to London especially for him.

Now turn to the right and walk a few yards back to the cross in High Cross.

This is the end of the walk but the cathedral is worth visiting and has guides willing to show you round. The cathedral has a restaurant in the chapter house and Truro Methodist has a restaurant just inside the main doors, appropriately called Sambells. Of course there is much that you have not seen but a thousand years of history has unrolled before you. Let us hope that much of what you have seen can be preserved for future generations.

Bibliography

Great Western Rail, Resource Pack.

Ashley Rowe – *Some Chapters in Truro History*

John Betjeman & A.L.Rowse – *Victorian & Edwardian Cornwall from Old Photographs*

A.L.Rowse – *Tudor Cornwall*

'J.H.C.' – *History of Cornwall 1893*

F.E. Halliday – *A History of Cornwall*

H.L. Douch – *The Book of Truro*

Truro Buildings Research Group

Viv Acton – *A History of Truro, Volume I*

R.S. Best – *The Life & Good Works of John Passmore Edwards*

Burrow's Guide – *Truro Cathedral*

Dean & Chapter – *Historical & Architechtural Notes of Truro Cathedral*

Arthur Lyne – *Around Truro in Old Photographs*

G.C. Bamfield, OBE – *St Clement, the church of Moresk*

Valerie Brokenshire – *A Parish Portrait, St Blazey*

Walter H. Tregellas – *Cornish Worthies*

W.J. Burley – *City of Truro 1877 – 1977*

Index